Unless the
LORD

A book about trusting the Lord through Psalm 127

Alan Gedde

ISBN 978-1-68517-208-4 (paperback)
ISBN 978-1-68517-209-1 (digital)

Christian Faith Publishing, Inc.
832 Park Avenue
Meadville, PA 16335
www.christianfaithpublishing.com

Printed in the United States of America

Contents

Acknowledgments

I would like to thank all those who made it possible for this book to be written:

- My wife, Tamra, who endured many hours of verbal processing and continued to encourage me to write this book. In fact, she has spent the last thirty years being my biggest fan.
- All of my six children—Harmony, Maryruth, Elsie, Nehemiah, Phoebe, and Cora—making my life an adventure and keeping me honest.
- My family. They are mentioned a lot. They have loved me through all the good and bad.
- My church. Not only did they encourage me to write the book, but also gave me the time to do it.

Introduction

The world today is harsh, challenging for the average person to make it. Suicide is at an all-time high, divorce rates continue to hover, around 50 percent, and child-adult relationships seem more fractured than ever. It truly is hard to live in today's day and age, or is it? I was born in the seventies and grew up in the eighties. My dad was born during the forties and grew up in the fifties. My grandpa was born before 1910 and grew up in the twenties. I know a lot of people who like to say, "Life was easier then."

"Life was better then."

The truth is I have said it. I often talk to my kids about the joys I had of never being at home because I was outside all the time. I forget to mention the things that were not so good. It was not easy to be a kid in any of these decades or an adult.

As a child, I lived in a small suburban town. Almost all of my friends came from homes where their parents were divorced. Those that weren't divorced were on the verge. To my knowledge, only one of my friends' parents stayed together until just recently when his father passed. Did you catch that? One.

I had three high school acquaintances commit suicide either during high school or shortly after, and many of my friends had fractured relationships with at least one of their parents. So, I think it might be possible to say that the eighties weren't much better than now. I think you might be able to go right down the list of decades and find that although on the surface it might have been better to look at, under the surface was the same turmoil that we see today.

What if the problem of all our generations is not the state of the world but the state of the heart? It is with this idea that I decided I wanted to tackle some things in a book. I, for years, have wondered why I believe the things I did about marriage, about parenting, about finances—heck—about everything. This book will take a hard look at the misconceptions I had as a kid and as an adult about all areas of life. I wanted to use a passage that I always loved but never followed—a passage that Tamra, my wife, showed me very early on in our marriage. A passage that we have built our marriage and lives around. That passage is Psalm 127.

Psalm 127

A song of ascents. Of Solomon.
Unless the Lord builds the house,
the builders labor in vain.
Unless the Lord watches over the city,
the guards stand watch in vain.
In vain you rise early
and stay up late,
toiling for food to eat—
for He grants sleep to those He loves.
Children are a heritage from the Lord,
offspring a reward from him.
Like arrows in the hands of a warrior
are children born in one's youth.
Blessed is the man
whose quiver is full of them.
They will not be put to shame
when they contend with their opponents in court.

Tamra and I have tried to follow this verse. Truly, she does better at it than me. Throughout our lives together there are multiple times that we have had to truly live by the words "unless the Lord." Those times have been some of the most difficult and some of the most wonderful. Those words, "unless the Lord," are a foundation to what I believe is the foundation of our marriage. When Tamra first introduced it to me, I liked it because it talked about arrows and children; of course, it means so much more than that. I think it might have a lot to say to us today concerning how we should live our lives. I plan on taking you through this passage in hopes that it will encourage you to live life with a purpose far greater than the world has to offer, a purpose that will continue for generations and bring light to the world around us.

If you have picked up this book in hopes of self-help—good, I think it can although that help might look different from what you think. The type of help this book offers comes in the form of a loving relationship with a heavenly Father. This book will help you see just how much you can depend on him.

Finally, if you picked up this book and never asked Jesus to be your Lord and Savior, let me tell you how you can fix that right now. You can fix that by a pretty simple process—a process that starts by realizing there is a heaven and a hell. You see, heaven is a real place, a place paved with golden streets where everyone is praising Jesus, and there are no more tears, no more pain, and no more worries.

There is a problem though—that problem is sin. Sin is anything we do that doesn't follow God's laws and therefore separates us from God. The Bible says that everyone is a sinner. Romans 3:23 states that all have sinned and fall short of the glory of God. Because of that sin, we are eternally separated from God. But God loves us and doesn't want to be separated from us. He wants to be close to us, so God sent his Son, Jesus, down to earth where he lived a perfect life, a life without sin. Jesus then had to pay the penalty for our sins. Jesus died on the cross and took our punishment so that we could be granted closeness with God. He then rose on the third day to show his power over death.

Because of this, we can be close to God, but we must accept his gift. The first thing you do—admit that you are a sinner. The Bible says in Romans 3:23 that all have sinned and fall short of the glory of God. Not one person in this world can claim they are without sin, which is just a fact. The Bible also says in Romans 6:23 that the punishment of sin is death. So you must first admit that you are a sinner.

After acknowledging that you are a sinner, you can ask God to forgive you of your sin. Then you ask to accept God's gift of salvation.

Romans 5:8 declares, "But God demonstrates His own love toward us, in that while we were still sinners, Christ died for us." Romans 10:9 says, "that if you confess with your mouth Jesus as Lord, and believe in your heart that God raised Him from the dead, you will be saved." Romans 10:13 repeats it: "For everyone who calls on the name of the Lord will be saved." If you are willing to ask Jesus to forgive you of your sins, believe that he is Lord and that he did that and ask him to come and be your savior, would you pray this prayer right now? Saying this prayer is a way to declare to God that you rely on Jesus Christ for your salvation. The words themselves will not save you. Only faith in Jesus Christ can provide salvation!

> God, I know that I have sinned against you and am deserving of punishment. But Jesus Christ took the punishment that I deserve so that through faith in him, I could be forgiven. With your help, I place my trust in you for salvation. Thank you for your wonderful grace and forgiveness—the gift of eternal life! Amen!

I hope you prayed that prayer, but if you didn't, that is okay. Continue reading. I believe that this book will be fun for you to read, and maybe after reading it, you might want to come back to this page and pray that prayer. I hope you enjoy this book as much as I enjoyed writing it.

Alan Gedde

Chapter 1

My Journey

You know the memory, the one that is forever stuck in your brain, the one you are sure is incorrect but no matter how often you try and recall it, it is always the same? Yeah, that one. Mine happened when I was three (I think). We were hunting in Oregon with my sister Elaine, my mom, and Iva Chrisman. That is right—one of my first hunting memories is of two women and a girl hunting. My sister was twelve or thirteen, so she was a little girl. To my knowledge, this is the only memory I have of my mom hunting. I have some memories of her being in camp, but not many since my parents were divorced when I was only five years old; but I am sure she was out there supporting her daughter with one of her best friends, Iva. Let me take some time here to talk about these three ladies, and it's important because the people in our lives make us who we are.

My mom, Diane, is a real trooper. At five-feet-nothing, she has been through a lot and survived. In my life, I don't remember a time when she wasn't my biggest cheerleader—well, okay, maybe once. Let me share. When I was a young worship pastor at a small Southern Baptist church, I decided to sing "In the Garden" with a bit of pep. At the end of the song, the church seemed to enjoy it, but when an elderly gentleman from the congregation approached me later that week and told me I was playing the devil's game and that I had ruined a great old hymn, I was shocked. I called my mom and told her what was happening, and she said to me that she would box my ears if she were with me. I guess that is still supporting. My mom showed up at every concert, game, and every other thing I did because that is who she is even if it meant a significant cost to her. She worked her tail off. I was a latchkey kid because Mom was working and didn't have the money to pay for childcare, which brings me to Iva Chrisman. Iva was a friend of the family, one of those "dyed in the wool" friends of the family. She was tough, raising three rough boys; and she was kind, one of the most considerate women I have ever met.

When Mom needed something, Iva was there. She ended up babysitting me for quite a while. But the story I remember most about Iva and my mom happened when I was probably eight or nine. My mom had received some devastating news on a particular day— news that the man she had been dating had died of a heart attack. I remember it because I don't think I had ever seen my mom cry so hard. I was too young to understand what was going on, but I remember Iva showing up to the apartment to spend the evening with mom while my brother and I watched the wrestling cage match down at the high school. Iva has since gone to be with Jesus, but what she meant to my family and me is priceless.

Then there is my sister Elaine. Elaine is ten years older than me, but I never questioned whether she loved her little brother. Much like my mom, Elaine supported all my endeavors. Her husband, Jeff, my brother from another mother, would show up at all my football games, coaching me from the sidelines, "Stay home! Stay home!" When Jeff and Elaine started dating, I was young enough that it is hard not to mention them in the same breath. I was not easy to live with for her either; I was the snotty kid she had to babysit. When I was very young, she wouldn't let me vacuum; when I threw a fit, she sent me to my bedroom.

Instead of going to my room, I went to my parents' room. They had a headboard that reached the window. I climbed up on the headboard, opened the window, and ran away. When I was very young, we lived in a little ranch house way off the beaten path. We were the only house on Greenleaf Drive that I can remember, and it was quite a walk to get the mail. Elaine saw me leaving, and when she asked me where I was going, I told her I would check the mail. She was probably fourteen, maybe fifteen, and was done with me. It was quite a ways down that road, so it wasn't anything for her to let me go. I am sure she had no idea what I would do next.

The mailboxes were actually beside a major highway. I went to that highway and started walking. I walked to a place called Shorty's Corner, which is probably a couple of miles away. Just in case you are wondering, that is a long and dangerous way for a four- or five-year-old to go. When I walked into the store, the nice lady behind the counter told me to come behind the counter and play with her child. There were toys there, so I played.

Meanwhile, she called my mom. Needless to say, when my mom arrived, I became frightened. I crawled to the back of the car behind the back seat, where my mom couldn't reach me, and she drove me home. I don't know what happened after that. It could be that the trauma was too significant and I have buried it, but I am guessing that the trauma was worse for my sister because she was probably worried sick—at least I hope she was. Anyway, Elaine is a super sister, and I have never once doubted her love for me.

So here we were walking down a dirt road. There were six of us. Iva's children, Bill and Steve, were hanging out with me quite a ways back of the three ladies. I have hunted with kids long enough now that I am sure we were loud and not paying any attention. All of a sudden, stuff started to happen. My sister fired her gun. By some miracle, a little forked horn buck had sat out in an opening long enough for my older sister to shoot it. (My dad has told me several times that he seems to have a lot of luck when he has kids with him. I agree. I have had some pretty good luck with my kids as well.) So the gun went off, and I was awakened from my three-year-old brain that something marvelous had just happened. I don't recall the events clearly because of my age, but I went from laughing to hearing a gun go off. What happened next was the most vivid part of the memory I have.

We all walked down to where the deer was, and it was still breathing. I remember thinking it was going to come back to life, which caused me a little fear. Someone had to finish off the deer, and

I recollect that Iva did that. I could be wrong, but that is my recollection. What had started as a fun event turned into a bit of a situation. It was a thirteen-year-old girl, my mom, three little boys, and Iva. Iva, a well-adapted outdoors person, was ready to get to work, which meant a knife and some blood. So my mom would get my dad and bring him and Big Bill back to get the deer back to camp. Big Bill was Iva's husband. I remember him as a mountain of a man who was always gentle. He loved to hunt, loved his boys, and was one of my dad's best friends.

I waffled. In my memory, this exchange took a while but probably was a little quicker than I remember. It went something like this: Mom asked, "Alan, are you coming with me or not?" I wanted to go. Fear of what was happening with the deer scared me, but having to go with Mom and miss out on being with Bill and Steve scared me just as much. So I wavered between the yes and the no for what seemed like an eternity. Finally, out of frustration, my mom grabbed my hand, and off we went. I remember how my mom was going very fast, and I felt like I was flying through the air, my feet barely touching the ground, only every once in a while. As I think back on it now, my mom probably wasn't running, but I was three; I am sure I looked like some ragdoll flopping through the air, trying to keep up as best I could. That is the end of the memory. Through the years, I have been able to fill in the rest of the story. We found dad driving down the road in his 1970s purple Toyota Land Cruiser that he called Plum Crazy. He called it Plum Crazy because, at one point, he decided he wanted to paint it purple—that's right, purple. For the rest of my childhood, dad loved the term plum crazy. I remember his bowling teams were consistently named Plum Crazy.

I have often wondered why this memory stands so clear in my mind. I don't remember many other things that happened on that trip, and I don't know many other memories from that time in my childhood—at least not that clearly. It wasn't a particularly traumatic event although seeing the dying deer breathing, I guess, was slightly traumatic. I didn't shoot the deer, so I don't think it holds much in the way of a milestone event. After pondering this thought for many years, I believe I have pegged why it sticks. This memory is the only memory I have where my parents were married.

My mom and dad were divorced when I was five, so I don't remember much about them being married. I have pictures, people have shared stories with me, but memories—none except this one. I believe that this memory is an important one for a lot of reasons. It is the only memory of my parents being married. It was my first experience seeing an animal dead, and it was my first experience hunting. As I look at who I am now, I know how this memory has shaped me in so many ways.

You might be asking why you would start a book about Psalm 127 with this story? Really, this is my first memory and who I am is linked to this memory. How I view Psalm 127 finds its roots right here in this memory. Before I dive into some of that, let me explain.

I am a Christ follower. When I was sixteen years old, Jesus and his story changed my life. My family didn't go to church, so I didn't know Jesus. I knew who he was. I had heard some good country Western songs that talked about him, knew some people in high school that went to Younglife and had even gone a couple of times myself because of a girl. I will expound on all of those things later, but for now, know that Jesus did change my life in a very dramatic fashion.

I am a husband. When I was twenty years old, I married the love of my life, Tamra; and after twenty-nine—years of marriage and six children, I don't see the train coming to a halt anytime soon. Being a husband is a badge I wear proudly for several reasons, but time, experience, and years of study have caused me to be very different than what I thought a husband was supposed to be. Again, I will expound on these things later, but now know that I am a husband.

I am a father. I have six children—that is right, six: five daughters and one son. At the time of writing this, they range in age from twenty-seven to five. They are the reason I hope I can sell some copies of this book. I need the extra cash! Being a father is a blessing but one that comes with many challenges. I have done an excellent job at times, and I have failed miserably at times. I will talk about all of those as we go through this book, but know this—I am a father.

Finally, I am a hunter. Hunting is not just a part of my life; it is part of my DNA. I learned how to hunt early in life. I have success stories, and I have failure stories. I will talk about many of these stories throughout this book and how they relate to my end goal. Know this, though—I am a hunter.

These are essential factors as you begin to read this book. My goal will be to show you how Psalm 127 and other passages in the Bible changed my total views on Christianity, marriage, and parenting. The hunting stories will be a fun way of helping you understand how all that we do, every little thing, can weave our lives together to create something unique.

Why Psalm 127?

I don't remember the first time that Psalm 127 struck me, but I think it was my first or second year in New Mexico. I moved to New Mexico in 2003 to be a youth and music pastor at a small Southern Baptist church. How I got here was quite a feat.

Tamra and I had felt called to be missionaries; we thought God had called us to a life of service overseas. So on a Sunday morning, we took a step of faith and committed to giving our life on the mission field. Our pastor gave us instructions on how to start the process, and we started. The first thing we had to do was call the mission organization. The call was not what we expected. The mission organization told us that they would love for us to be missionaries, but I, husband, needed the degree, not the wife. (This was the first time since I had decided to follow Jesus that I questioned the church. How could this rule be there? My wife was clearly the smart one, and she had such a firm hold on his Word. This seemed wrong.) Since I did not have my degree, we decided it would be a while until we were missionaries because going back to school didn't seem possible.

I was working at a lawn care company and had been doing well there. I had more responsibility, so things were going well. I was happy, I was earning a good living, and we had a lovely house. Our children were in excellent schools, and we had a great church group. We were living the good life, and I couldn't see how school was going to help. Also, and maybe this was the overriding factor, I was a terrible student. I tried college out when I was younger, and I struggled a lot! When Tamra and I got married, I decided to work and for Tamra to go to college. It worked very well. I was successful, and Tamra was working as a school teacher. So college just didn't seem doable, and I couldn't wrap my head around it.

The problem was that we had committed to this and still felt God continually pushing in that direction. I would be reminded of this commitment by friends, by my pastor, and of course, by Tamra; she always reminded me that God would not have called us if he didn't have a plan. Then there was this overriding guilt where I just knew that I wasn't supposed to spend the rest of my life making sure people's landscapes were green and weed-free. In the spring of 1998, I drew a deer tag that I had wanted since I had lived in Arizona. I was very excited. This area of the state had produced some huge bucks, and I had a coveted rifle tag in November. I put in for my vacation time and started scouting the area. One of those scouting trips produced a lesson I will never forget.

Harmony and I left one morning to go down and learn the area, find a place to camp, and see where I would hunt. The road was pretty good except for some rocky washes. In one of the steeper washes, someone had put railroad ties in to make it easier for a vehicle to get through it. I didn't have a problem going in, so it made sense that this wouldn't be a big deal.

As I began to go up the wash heading out, I flipped one of the railroad ties and was high centered on the side of a hill, definitely not ideal. So here I was, stuck in the middle of nowhere with my five-year-old daughter. Cell service was limited, so we were stuck, and I was alone in figuring out how to get out of this situation. I couldn't see a safe way out, so I went the dangerous route. I made sure the emergency brake was on, got the small jack out of the back seat, and began lifting the axle far enough off the ground so I could remove the railroad tie. I got it high enough, crawled under the truck, and kicked the railroad tie out from under the axle. The whole time, Harmony was over on a rock just enjoying herself; occasionally, she would say something to me.

I was successful. With the railroad tie removed, I was able to get us out of that wash. I remember feeling very proud of myself, and in my mind, I was quite the man. It was at this point that Harmony said, "Dad, I was praying the whole time that God would help us, and he did. God saved us, Dad." Leave it to a five-year-old to humble you. Anyway, with scouting done and vacation days planned, I was ready for the hunt.

In September, my boss approached me with some bad news. He called me into his office and said, "Alan, I know that you have requested these dates off, and you have earned those days, but the company has decided to do a big sales/production event on that weekend, and I need you here."

It was not a hard decision. I told him, "Well, I will not be here. This is the only weekend I can hunt there, and the tag is only good for that weekend."

I continued to discuss how the hunting world works, how drawing a tag can take years and that the state doesn't care if you can't hunt that weekend. You don't go; you lose the chance.

My boss seemed concerned, and he pleaded with me to see if it was at all possible to change the weekend. I decided to do some research and found a loophole. I could change my hunt! I could forfeit my rifle hunt for an archery hunt in January. January is when the deer in my part of the country where I live are in rut, making them a little easier to bow hunt. I began to research what I would need to do to make that hunt happen. How much would a bow and arrow setup cost? What about lessons? Would I need more time?

After about a week, I took my findings to my supervisor. I told him that I could change the hunt, but that meant he would have to do some stuff. I told him I would need the money for a new bow set up, which includes everything necessary to hunt. I included a case and some camo clothing in my estimate. I then said I would need another week of vacation to accomplish this task; finally, I would want to use the company truck, and the company would pay for gas. He was more than happy to meet my demands, so began my journey into archery hunting. (By the way, it is stuff like this that has compelled my wife to identify me as a master schmoozer.)

A small archery store was not too far from home that I could buy my bow and learn the basics of shooting. They had a small range there so that I would go every day at lunch and shoot. I started to become pretty good and felt confident that I could shoot an animal at forty yards. I became pretty excited as the days drew closer for my hunt; I could picture the large mule deer bucks across the cactus-scattered hills in the coveted Chiracaua mountains.

The life-changing hunt

I left my home Friday after work to take the four-hour drive to the spot I had picked for camp. I got to my campsite about 9:00 a.m. and started setting up camp. I remember taking my time and just enjoying the fact that I had made it. I was on a solo hunt with my bow, and it felt great. After getting everything set up, I took time to sit in the shade of the tree close by and glass some of the hills nearby. I wasn't expecting to see anything, and then he appeared. He was one of the most beautiful bucks I had ever seen. He was lying next to a pretty large boulder, and from where I was sitting, he looked asleep; he was probably a good mile away although it was hard for me to judge. I grabbed my pack, my bow, and took off. I could see an excellent way to get close enough to shoot this majestic buck, maybe possibly.

I walked over to the canyon behind the buck and started up where I thought he was lying. It was a lot steeper than it looked. I slowly and methodically worked my way up to the top of the ridge, where I thought I would be right on top of this buck. I peeked over the hill—no buck. I looked and looked, and I couldn't see him anywhere! Where had he gone? I took my binoculars out and started glassing again. There he was! He looked as far away as he did before! I had misjudged and climbed up the wrong ridge! I was frustrated, but there wasn't anything I could do about it now. The light was starting to fade, and I wanted to make sure I was back at camp before it got too dark. I got back to camp, made my dinner and ate, and started to read my Bible. I had decided that I would read through Matthew while I was on this trip—something I had never done.

I woke up the following day and decided to see if that buck was still in the area. He was! I spent the whole day trying to get close to that buck and hunted harder than I ever had. I never did close the gap. I did get chased by a very mean steer, which was quite frightening because I was pretty sure my bow wasn't going to stop him. I was able to find a fence and get underneath it fast enough that he couldn't get to me. That experience pretty much ended my hunt for him, and I went back to camp empty-handed and tired.

That night I continued my reading through Matthew, and I got to Matthew 4:18–20 (NIV):

> As Jesus was walking beside the Sea of Galilee, he saw two brothers, Simon called Peter and his brother Andrew. They were casting a net into the lake, for they were fishermen. "Come, follow me," Jesus said, "and I will send you out to fish for people." At once, they left their nets and followed him.

This passage hit me hard. I knew we were called to be missionaries, but I just couldn't wrap my head around the concept that I could or should go back to college for all the reasons I mentioned earlier. But here I was reading about men who had just cast their nets into the lake, and they just left them. I read that verse again and again and again. They just left their nets. I felt moved by that thought and began to reevaluate what that meant for me and for what God had called me to do. It didn't take long for me to realize that God asked me to do the same thing—to drop my nets and follow him into a life of ministry. I lay down, and after several minutes of prayer, I was able to drift off to sleep.

I was awakened in the middle of the night by something outside my tent. Something had its nose up against my tent and was sniffing. I didn't know what to do precisely. I didn't know what it was. Was it a cow? A coyote? A bear? A mountain lion? I just didn't know, and I froze. I just lay there in my sleeping bag, praying that whatever it was wouldn't eat me. (Okay, this is not one of my proudest moments as a hunter and a man. I was terrified. I look back at it and cringe—what a wimp.) After about fifteen minutes, whatever it was walked away, presumably because it decided I wouldn't taste very good. I had a tough time sleeping the rest of the night, and to this day, I don't know what was sniffing around my tent; however, I still feel like a big wimpy baby when I tell the story.

I didn't sleep much, so when my alarm rang, I was ready to get up and be done with this night. I was exhausted and didn't feel much like walking all over the desert, trying to find deer. I had had quite a night, and God had got me thinking and then my visitor. I decided to drive the truck down to an area with more trees and some prettier country. I took my time and occasionally glassed to see what was out there. I turned into the canyon, which was very pretty. There was a little picnic area off to my right, and I was going to pull in and check it out when three deer crossed the road right in front of my truck. The last deer was a little buck, and when I say little, I mean tiny. These were Coues deer, not mule deer, and this little buck was barely legal. They all stopped next to one of the picnic tables. I grabbed my bow, stepped to the front of the truck, and shot. I hit him! He walked away into some long grass.

I pulled my truck off into the picnic area and started looking for the buck. I couldn't find the buck. I could see the blood. I even found my arrow, and it was covered in blood, but I could not find that buck. About thirty minutes into my search, some guys came by in trucks and asked how things were going. I told them what happened, and they helped me look for that little buck. After a long search, we determined that I probably missed the vitals and shot a little low. I was disappointed. They invited me over to their camp, ate, hung out, and learned some things about the area. It was a great afternoon, but my hunt was over. I had read enough articles about ethical archery hunting that I knew that I needed to notch my tag. Even if that little buck had lived, I had shot something and not recovered it, and it is one of the drawbacks of archery hunting.

That night I slept better, and the following day I got up, broke down camp, and went back to see if I could find that little buck.

After a few hours and many miles, I gave up looking and started the long drive home.

I spent the drive home going through the conversation I was going to have with Tamra. God had shared with me that I needed to leave the nets. That meant I needed to quit my job and go back to school. I knew that this meant we would have to change our lives drastically, and how were we going to be able to do that? How could I quit work? It was my job to provide for my wife and kids. How would people look at me? What would they think?

I reached the street in front of my house, walked in my home's front door, and Tamra was sitting there in the front room. After we greeted each other, I told her that God had given me clear direction and that I needed to quit work and go back to school full-time. Without even blinking an eye, Tamra said it was about time. She clearly had never wavered, as usual; she continued to believe that God was in control and that, eventually, I would listen. So the next step in this journey began.

A true Provider

The next few months were a blur. I had a lot of work to do, and there was the task of finding where I would go to school, quitting a successful job, figuring out how we would be able to keep our house, and still maintaining the household finances. The tasks at hand seemed daunting, and they were. I'll skip over the gory details, but I chose to go to a local Christian school and study ministry as my degree with many prayers and thought. I was able to get a few scholarships and enough financial aid to make it all work, but I still wasn't making any money. The situation was my first experience in working through some of my expectations as a husband and father.

I started school and began the process of looking for work; meanwhile, the money in savings had dried up, and we were looking at more bills than we had money. I was desperately seeking a job but was having no luck. The first blow to my ego was when we realized we would need to sell the house. Tamra and I talked about it and prayed about it, but in the end, I just couldn't get past the idea that

I was not providing for my family so my children wouldn't have a home to live in. I remember in one of our conversations, I was telling Tamra just how much I would need to make for us to be able to rent a place, and she responded by saying, "I'm praying God will provide a place for free."

I know I didn't laugh out loud, but I believed that would happen for about a millisecond. My real-world brain didn't allow for such foolishness. Of course, I'm sure you have already guessed, but that is what ended up happening. Give me a second before I share that story. I was in a bad place. You see, I had grown up in a world that said it was my job to provide and protect for my family, and I was failing. To make ends meet, we needed to ask for help from family and even went to the food bank a couple of times. I was devastated that I was doing this to my family. My ego was taking a hit. It was during this time that I started looking at some things. This was when Tamra really helped me focus on Psalm 127. She never wavered. Her faith was strong because she truly believe that "unless the Lord"—there would be no other reason for doing what we were doing. I promise I will get to the passage, but let me continue the story; it will all come together later.

The school I attended in Phoenix had a ministry fair. Every student was required to serve in a ministry for an allotted amount of time per week. I knew that it was all volunteer, and I wondered how I would juggle family, job, school, and ministry; but I went to the fair, hoping to get plugged in. One of the booths there was a ministry called Apartment Life. Apartment Life is a ministry where you minister to the apartment communities. I was very intrigued. I was an apartment kid. I grew up and lived in varying sizes of apartment buildings for a substantial part of my childhood. I just couldn't help but think this ministry would be a good fit for me. What I didn't know was that Apartment Life didn't want you coming in and helping. They wanted you to live in the apartment, and they provided the apartment for you! Ta da! Not only that, but it was not just a ministry for me, it was for us. I would not be doing this alone; Tamra would be ministering right beside me, and the children would be ministering as well. I was shocked! Dismayed! Hopeful! For the first time in a while, I saw the light at the end of the tunnel. Not only light, but this would be a chance for us to do mission work right where we already lived; it was a match made in heaven.

There was an immediate connection between the director of the Phoenix area ministry and us, and we could both see that God was moving in a compelling way for us to move in this direction. It did not take long to get the ball rolling. Of course, we still needed to sell our house and still had many other bills, but we were able to sign on to Apartment Life after a few weeks.

It was a pretty incredible few weeks. God moved quickly and established that he was working through this in a pretty cool way. Our house sold quickly and for the asking price, which allowed us to pay off debt and even get a more practical car. The apartment needing a couple was in Mesa and wasn't one of the high-end apartment complexes, so they were willing to give us a two-bedroom without any rise in cost instead of the standard one-bedroom, which was a huge blessing because we had two daughters. These events and many others are how we began my school years. Through these years, I learned to be more dependent on God; I realized that God and only God is the provider and protector of my family. I began to take Psalm 127 a little more seriously.

My salvation

I have alluded that my upbringing led me to believe some things, and I would like to dive into that a little bit before moving forward here. I grew up in a relatively average family. My mom and dad were divorced when I was five years old. Although that situation might not be typical for many, it was my normal. I have a sister that is ten years older than me, a brother that is seven years older than me, and a younger brother that is ten years younger than me. In many ways, I was an only child. I spent a lot of time on my own—not that I was miserable. I just was left to my own devices a lot. After the divorce, Mom had to work full-time, and my brother and sister were quite a bit older, so there were many days that I was doing my own thing. I learned how to cook for myself pretty early on, and I was adept at taking care of myself. So many things occurred during these times, and many of them formed my belief system. I don't believe that anyone taught me what to think; it was by default. Societal norms and a lot of television taught about who I was and who I was supposed to be.

From the ages of five to eleven, I lived with my mom in Sandy, Oregon. At that time, Sandy was a thriving metropolis of four thousand people. I spent my summers playing baseball, swimming, and staying out until dark. Sandy is a little town at the base of Mount Hood. You could say that everybody knew everybody and you wouldn't be a liar. Sandy was a wonderful place to grow up. As children, there were times we wouldn't be inside a house for days except to sleep. For illustration purposes, a bank in Sandy had a great hill for skateboarding that we liked to use a lot.

We would spend hours out there just hanging out, riding different devices down the hill, and scraping up knees. One day, one of my friends dared me to moon the drive-thru lady at the bank. For those who might live under a rock and don't know what that is, my friends asked me to pull down my pants and show this poor lady my bare white bottom. I was hesitant initially but then decided I wasn't a wimp and gave the lady the full moon. We ran away, laughing at the thought of this lady having to stare at my rear. We thought we were so sly. I don't remember how old I was, but when my mom came home from work that day, she told me she received a phone call from someone who had told her what I had done. I didn't get in trouble, but my mom was pretty stern that I didn't do that anymore.

So, you can see that Sandy was a pretty small place. It was also a great place. Any time I reminisce about those days, there are very few bad memories. I had so much fun as a child growing up in that great little town. However, in those fun times, I began to develop a sense of how life was supposed to look. I developed a sense of what a healthy family looked like and what an unhealthy family looked like. I met people who encouraged me to be more than I could. I developed what I would consider a blueprint for what my family would and would not be.

When I was eleven years old, I moved in with my dad. He lived in Portland, Oregon, so it was a significant change for me. I went from being a big fish in a little pond to being the new kid in the big city. I struggled a lot in the first year. I hadn't ever had to make friends. All of my friends in Sandy were my neighbors and school buddies who I knew my whole life. All of a sudden, I was thrust into a situation that I had to make friends. I was the country bumpkin from the little town, and I didn't dress right; I didn't act right. It was tough, but things did get better especially when dad decided to move in with my grandma and grandpa.

We spent a couple of years with my grandma and grandpa. It was a different situation for me. When I came home from school, Grandma was at home, and she always had a snack waiting for me. My grandma was a wonderful little lady. When I say little, I am not exaggerating. Her name was Elsie, and she was probably four feet six inches tall; but she was tough, and she was sweet. She was one of the hardest-working women I have ever known. I don't think I remember her sitting down very often. She was always moving. Even if she was watching TV, she was moving. My favorite memories of her are her standing in front of the TV, clapping in rhythm to the music. She was a great teacher as well.

Her cupboards were always full of goodness. One of the things she always had on stock was semi-sweet chocolate chips. One time, I decided that I would rather have the semi-sweet chocolate chip bag with me in my room, so when no one was looking, I swiped a bag and took it to my room. I put the bag in the top drawer of my dresser—probably not the most intelligent place to hide them, considering my grandma did my laundry. I hadn't thought that through, though, so I was excited to have that snack whenever I wanted.

Grandma was a master though. She had raised three boys and had me pegged. Rather than scold me, Grandma just stopped making snacks for after school. When I think back on it, Grandpa probably wasn't too happy with me either; he always got to enjoy the afternoon snacks as well. It didn't take long for me to ask the dumb question: "Hey, Grandma, how come we don't have any snacks?"

Her response, "Well, I have wanted to make some cookies, but I don't have any chocolate chips." She stared at me over the frames of her glasses.

I knew I was had. I walked down to my room, grabbed what was left, and brought them back. Grandma was not mad; she took the chocolate chips back and said, "Let that be a lesson to you." End of the story; she never talked about it again. Grandma was that way. She just expected better, and she usually got better.

Grandpa usually was outside, working in the yard or watching an old Western on TV. I loved living with them, and as I look back, these were super times. Living with them also added some wrinkles into the fabric of my future. This was the first time I lived with a married couple that I considered happy. These two truly loved each other—warts and all. I began to love classic country music, and I began to love coffee and doughnut time. Most of all, it caused me to look at what a healthy family looked like in a different light.

We eventually moved out of my grandparents' home into a home that my dad and his girlfriend, my future extraordinary step-mom Lorraine, bought just right up the road. It was at this house I developed some different habits. I started high school; my dad had a new toddler running around, and I was left on my own again. I don't want to get into too much of what that did, but I acted a lot like a high school boy with no limits or rules. These were also good times but not ones that I relish. However, there was a group of us in that neighborhood that began hanging out. We played a lot of basketball.

One day, Steve invited me to church. I had no desire to go to church. The people I knew who went to church were friendly, but they were not *my* kind of people. They had too many rules and not enough fun. After some convincing, I decided to go to Wednesday night basketball. It was there that I met Jim Fitzpatrick, who was a young youth pastor at a small church down the road from my house. Every Wednesday night, he would share how much Jesus loved me and how I could accept his gift of forgiveness. On June 7, 1989, I drove home from that message and could feel that I needed to do something. That night, I kneeled next to my bed and asked Jesus to forgive me of my sins and come live in my heart. Although I didn't understand what that meant, I knew it was what I was supposed to do.

I think that I have given you quite a bit of history to this point, and I don't want to belabor the point more than I need to, but here is the *Reader's Digest* version for those of you who read this and didn't care. A good family raised me, I was loved, and I was cared for. One day, though, God chose me; and when he did, he changed my life, which brings me to this passage, Psalm 127:

> Unless the Lord builds the house,
> the builders labor in vain.
> Unless the Lord watches over the city,
> the guards stand watch in vain.
> In vain you rise early
> and stay up late,
> toiling for food to eat—
> for he grants sleep to those he loves.
> Children are a heritage from the Lord,
> offspring a reward from him.
> Like arrows in the hands of a warrior
> are children born in one's youth.
> Blessed is the man
> whose quiver is full of them.
> They will not be put to shame
> when they contend with their opponents in court.

This passage is our passage. Tamra and I have, to the best of our ability, always tried to live our lives with this passage as a foundation. This passage has caused us to make some decisions that others might not have made, but this passage has also been the bedrock of our lives. I can't begin to think of the strength of our marriage and our family without thinking of this passage. It has been such a part of our lives that I wanted to write a book about it. I plan to take you through this passage in a fun and exciting way, weaving it through hunting, the outdoors, and my history to share how each verse has related to my life. I hope you have as much fun on this journey as I have had writing about it.

Chapter 2

A Good Camp

Unless the Lord builds the house, the laborers build in vain.
—Psalm 127:1a

We left home in the late afternoon, all packed up and ready to go. The drive to our destination would take us a total of two and a half hours and would include a trek on one of the roughest roads I have ever had the privilege to drive on. I have a dear friend who calls this road the ascent to hell. It was the third week of September, and I had an elk tag, two of my best friends, Jim and Tom, and all of the equipment necessary to get the job done. We made the drive through the valleys, stopped for a small drink at the gas station, then made our way over the mountain to our road. I turned off the road and started up the mountain.

This time of the year in southern New Mexico is usually absolutely gorgeous. The summer monsoon has created a short-lived oasis all over the desert. All of the water tanks are full, and long grass grows where there was brown dirt only two months ago. It is my favorite time of the year in New Mexico. It is also the best time to chase the majestic elk. They are in full rut mode, making it a tad bit easier to find these critters. The bulls spend their time searching for cows and broadcasting to the entire forest where they are. The weather is warm during the day but cools off quite nicely as soon as the sun goes down. It is a perfect time.

I turned up the dirt road and headed toward camp, where we would call home for the next few days. We took our time enjoying the scenery, glassing some hillsides, and just enjoying each other's company. There are just some things not easily forgotten, and this drive was one of those moments. After crossing the national forest boundary, we pulled off to our parking spot, unloaded the ATV, loaded up our first trip, and headed up the road to our camping spot. We had decided driving the ATV up, and back three or four times would be easier on our bodies than one trip up in the truck. After getting everything up there, we started setting up camp. It was getting pretty late, so we just put the tent up and unpacked everything. We figured we would take tomorrow afternoon to finish up base camp after we hunted in the morning.

It was hard to sleep that night. The bulls were bugling all around us. I was awakened several times thinking, *Man, they are close. Tomorrow will be an awesome day. I can't wait!* I remember dreaming of big bulls coming to us as we called them in close enough to sling an arrow at them.

Morning came, and we were up and ready to give chase. We ate a small breakfast, talked through what the morning hunt would look like, and headed up Goat Mountain. Goat Mountain is aptly named. From camp, the walk to Goat Mountain is two miles up. There are many game trails, small flat meadows, and a lot of trees and deadfalls. It is an excellent elk location where the elk go and bed down for the day. The three of us started in the dark, going up the mountain, hoping to get ahead of the elk before they got to their bedding areas, which meant we had to move fast. After only a short distance, we heard our first bugle. It was a way off, but we didn't care. We were bound and determined to move full steam ahead.

We came to the first heavily used game trail and started to call. (Elk hunting in the fall is about calling the elk to you—or at least using your calls to get the bull to respond so you know where he is. I love hunting elk this way, so I call a lot. On this particular hunt, Jim and Tom were the ones doing the calling since I needed to be the one hunting.) Jim and Tom's first calls were successful, and several bulls bugled back, telling us where they were. None were particularly close, and it sounded like they were above us; so after having a small conversation, we chose a direction and went after the closest one.

All right, let me take a moment to talk about Jim and Tom. Here are two of the most amazing friends someone could have. When we first moved to Roswell, we had left many friends in Phoenix, and it was Jim, Tom, and their families that took us in. I will talk about them individually, but Jim and Tom were the driving force behind my successes as a new youth and music pastor. They ran sound, volunteered in the youth ministry, built elaborate stage designs for VBS, and sacrificed for the sake of Christ. So when it came to hunting buddies, there they were. Jim is an adventurer. He is always ready to climb the next mountain, and frankly, he can. He is a marine, so he has the ability, and he has the nerve to do it. Jim is also an engineer, so he was always ready to practice something new. Tom is not quite the athlete or the tackle anything sort of guy, but do you need a shirt? Tom will give you the one off his back. Do you need someone to help you build something? Tom has the tools. Together they make a heck of a team. More than a few times, I have called on them to help with a big project, but the biggest one was when I asked if they could build a swing set for my children. For the next three Saturdays, they were at the house, creating a great swing and slide that stand to this day.

So here we were, the three of us, heading up Goat Mountain, working on trying to call in some bulls. The walk was not easy because the farther you go up Goat Mountain, the steeper it gets. The elk were up high. We walked pretty hard to get close. After a couple of hours of chasing one particular bull, we were very close. We had closed the gap and felt very good about our chances when the wind shifted and took our scent right to him. He and his herd of cows blew out of there, making more noise than a freight train in the middle of the night. He was gone, and our morning hunt was also quickly fading. The temperature was warming up, and we were pretty darn tired, so we decided to rest. (Resting is one of my favorite parts of hunting especially when you can find a shady spot on the north-facing slope of a mountain, which we had located. The air was warming up, but the ground was still cool from the night before, so it was just a perfect time of rest.)

We rested for about thirty minutes, bugling every ten minutes or so to see if a bull would respond to us. The last bugle got a response, and we made a decision. Well, the two of us did anyway. As Jim and I discussed going after that bull, Tom expressed his disinterest in going. He said he would head to camp and wait for us to come back for lunch. We parted ways—Tom back to camp and Jim and me after the bugles.

Jim and I hunted pretty hard. We followed several bugles but were never able to close the gap, hunting at its finest, the chase, the struggle, and the failure. But it is the failure that makes success so much fun. Jim and I trekked through several canyons, fought off oak bush thickets, and walked along several ridges before we decided to head back to camp for lunch. We talked as we walked about how we would set up camp. We knew there was a decent chance of rain, so we wanted to make sure we had camp fully set up before that happened. We talked about where we would hunt this afternoon and how Tom was probably well rested after taking a fantastic nap while we worked all morning. After about six hours of hard work, we turned the corner heading toward camp.

As we crested the hill, it was immediately apparent that Tom had not been napping the whole time. Tom had fully set up a very lovely and comfortable camp, complete with an indoor kitchen, dining room, and all the amenities necessary for a great hunt. It was a great camp. It was such a blessing, and after the cordial thank yous, Jim and I went to teasing Tom about his wifelike qualities in camp. He took the teasing well, but the truth is that camp made for a great hunt. There is something about a great camp that brings joy to the heart of the hunter—a place to fill your stomach, rest, and fellowship so that you have the energy to climb canyons and run after whatever you are running after with all the power you can muster.

That particular hunt did not end in a harvest although it was a lot of fun, and the elk encounters were many. I could have shot an elk. Several cows were very close on that hunt, but I was bound and determined to shoot a bull. I did shoot at a bull, but I missed, which happens. I also experienced seeing the biggest bull I have ever seen on that hunt. On the afternoon before the last day of the hunt, Tom, Jim, and I decided to sit. We had some radios, so I went up to a water tank, and Jim and Tom stayed out in some openings, glassing for elk. If they spotted something, they were to radio me, and we would see if I could make a plan and shoot something.

I got to the water tank at about three in the afternoon and got settled. I took my pack off, moved some things around, and had a granola bar and a bottle of water. I had found a perfect set of three trees that were about forty yards from the tank and offered shooting opportunities all around. I sat there for a while, intermittently napping and just enjoying the scenery and the sounds that you only get from being outdoors. The action started happening about five-thirty. Behind me, I could hear cow calls; they sounded like they were from the trees, but I also could hear something in the brush behind me. I was sitting, so I couldn't see what it was, but I was pretty sure it was coming my way.

I waited and waited when all of a sudden, there he was, a small five-point bull headed to the tank, and he didn't even know I was there. I was able to get all set up for a shot. The bull worked slowly, and I had picked out a small spot that would make for a perfect shot. He crept along, and when he got to the location, I released my arrow. The arrow went right under him, and I had misjudged the distance. He spooked a little, but he still didn't know what had happened, so he went back in the brush and stood there. I moved a little, thinking maybe a better position was needed so that I could see him. He was fifty yards away, and it was going to be a tough shot; but if he moved just a bit, I would be able to get him. The thing was he kept looking up the hill, not down toward the tank. I thought it was odd, and we were just there, still for what seemed like a lifetime—him staring at the trees, me staring at him. Just then, the mountain came alive, and my bull ran off. Coming down the hill and through the trees was the biggest bull I had ever seen. He was a monster, and his antlers were so big it made his body look small.

As he ran, he was panting, almost grunting, but he was coming after my little bull and telling him to get away. He stopped at the edge of the trees about a hundred yards away, and his cows, about twelve of them, followed. I tried to call to see if he would come closer, but he was not interested. I watched and listened as he glunked a few times and moved his cows ahead of him back up the mountain. It was one of my favorite memories of hunting. I was close but not close enough to shoot at him—overall a great hunt, and I think camp had a hand in making it so.

A good camp takes a lot of work. My family takes the camp experience, especially elk camp, to a high level. My family knows how to do such a thing. The Gedde camp in Oregon is like the Ritz Carlton of camps. It is enormous, has two canvas tents put together, is large enough to sleep multiple full-grown men, has a full kitchen and a refrigerator tent. Where they hunt in Oregon is quite cold, so a cold tent is easy to establish. It takes days to set up camp fully, and that camp usually stays set up for several weeks—but it is a palace!

The goal of a hunting camp is simple—make it so that you are dry, warm, well-fed, and well rested. I think I can say the same thing about a home minus the hunting. A good home is a home that refreshes the soul and allows someone to rest, be comfortable, and prepare for the adventure that is life.

Cultural norms

In my life as a child, I had many different homes and houses. I lived in apartments, basements, and full houses. Each one was unique and had benefits and drawbacks. Each one had different styles of families, so in many ways, they were all unique. There was one way they were not unique, and that was this—they took a lot of work.

My family is all hard workers. I can't remember a time where my parents didn't work. My mom worked whatever job she could get to pay rent after she and Dad were divorced, and I remember the same thing about my dad. He always had a job. They are both hard workers, and that trait passed on to me. When Tamra and I were married, the amount of advice I received about what it takes to be a good husband was outlandish and confusing.

On one side, I had my family and my upbringing. My dad worked hard, but so did my mom, so that was a given. The advice from my family was all over the place. My grandpa's best advice was never to let my wife know the checkbook's balance because if she knew the balance, she would spend all the money that I had earned. I thought that was strange advice, considering my grandma was a bookkeeper. My dad believes that the best wife earned her living and would go hunting and fishing with me. (Tamra hates hunting with me, but she does love fishing. When our first daughter was only two or three months old, we went on a fishing trip with my dad. Tamra was nursing Harmony when she got a bite. She continued nursing Harmony and reeled in a trout. I don't think I ever saw my dad more proud of a daughter-in-law.) I think my mom was just worried we were too young. Even though Tamra and I were madly in love (and still are), my mom was concerned that I would not be able to provide for her.

In the church, the advice was similar but in a different way. The church's message to me was that it was the husband's job to provide for the family and protect them. Some verses supported it like 1 Timothy 5:8, which says, "But if anyone does not provide for *his* own, and especially for those of his household, he has denied the faith and is worse than an unbeliever" (NKJV). I set *his* in italics to emphasize that it is a male who must provide. In the NIV, it is stated a little differently. It says, "Anyone who does not provide for their relatives, and especially for their own household, has denied the faith and is worse than an unbeliever." Regardless of the interpretation, the church promoted a home that emphasized provision and protection on the man. So being a good young Christian, I believed that this was an important role that I was to play in my life.

Not only was there a distinct church way of doing things, but the world was pretty clear about it as well. The television shows I watched growing up gave off the same message. The man would go to work, work long, hard hours, and then come home to his wife and children, who lived in a beautiful home. It was the wife's job to stay home, raise the children, and cook very fabulous meals for the husband. I would say that this was a Hollywood stereotype, but I began to notice that many of our church families were living this way.

Tamra's family was this way. Her mom stayed home and cared for the house and the children, and Tamra's father left early in the morning, worked all day, and then came home. It was what attracted me to their family in the first place. It was the opposite of my family; they were a Christian household, so that must be the right way. From the perspective of a young man looking to marry into this family, it would be vital that I was ready to provide for and protect my wife and children. That was my job.

There were problems, though, and it didn't all fit. When I looked at my mom, a single woman most of my life, I didn't see someone who needed a man to provide for her. She struggled financially, but she would always find a way. I can't imagine the stress this put on her. I remember when my brother accidentally burned rice-a-roni, which upset my mom because she couldn't afford to buy more. I can't even imagine what type of stress that was, knowing you couldn't afford eighty-four cents.

I was not marrying a girl that wanted to stay at home. She is smart, more intelligent than me, for sure. She is a driven person. She has a desire always to do better and grow more. She is independent, she loves me deeply; and I guess in that way, she needs me, but she doesn't need me to provide for her. She has always held to the truth that God provides for her. Tamra follows her faith in ways that I wish I did. So there were problems. In the end, I did not have anything other than the voices that I allowed to speak into my life, so I entered marriage with the thought that it was my job to provide and protect my family.

As a young married couple, we moved and got involved in a church pretty quickly. The church continued to perpetuate the idea that I was the provider of my family. The men would help me to find connections to new opportunities, and Tamra was in school. I remember the pastor, a very nice man, asking me how long I would make Tamra work and go to school. I remember thinking I needed a job that would provide more, so I started selling cars. I loved selling cars and was quite good at it, but the hours were long, and weekends were required actually to make money. It was not an excellent job for a young married couple. One time, Tamra and I were supposed to go to the opera with her school. Tamra had gotten all dressed up and was excited about the evening. When she came to pick me up (we only had one car), I was in the middle of selling a car. The deal wouldn't close, and I needed the sale, so she sat in the lobby as I sold the car. The exchange took too long, and we didn't go to the opera. Tamra sat there the whole time, and she even smiled when it was all done and supported me even though we didn't get to go. Have I mentioned that she is a pretty amazing lady? That story still stings. I could have easily had someone else finish that deal and took half the value, but my drive to provide kept me there to get the full commission. Here is the kicker. I showed up the following day to see the car I had sold was parked at the lot. It seems the buyers had decided that they did not want the car after all—it is called buyer's remorse. I wish that I had not made that sale, and that was almost thirty years ago. The amount of stress caused by my conviction to be the provider of my family was high and caused other problems where I struggled with self-doubt and probably lingered on depression at times.

Biblical truth

Take a look at verse 1 of Psalm 127. It says,

> Unless the Lord builds the house,
> the builders labor in vain.
> Unless the Lord watches over the city,
> the guards stand watch in vain.

It changed how I viewed my life. After being raised and being told that it was my job to provide for my family and protect my family, this verse just slapped me in the face. "Unless the Lord builds the house, the builders labor in vain."

What a concept. Unless the Lord builds the house, I was taught that a good job built the house all my life. If I did everything I needed to do, worked hard, got a good job, and budgeted well, I could afford a house. You see, nowhere was God mentioned. I had gone to church and knew that God would provide all those things as long as I was faithful to him. Also, though, I needed to work hard, that God would only provide for those that worked hard. There are over forty verses in the Bible that refer to working hard and having success. This verse turned the thought upside down to me. All that I had learned was that *my* hard work would be what got me the blessing. Yet here in this verse, it says "unless."

What a great word—*unless*. As a parent, it is one of my favorite. I will take you to McDonald's unless you get in trouble. This verse clearly says that God is my provider. God is the one that does the building and the providing. There is nothing I could do to accomplish the task as well as God could.

There are far more verses that show how God is the provider and so many stories, but one of my favorites is in Genesis 22. In this story, we see Abraham, the father of nations, tested by God. You see, Abraham had a son named Isaac, a son who Abraham had waited over one hundred years to have. Isaac was an answer to a promise God made Abraham. In this story, Abraham is asked by God to sacrifice his son:

> Then God said, "Take your son, your only son, whom you love—Isaac—and go to the region of Moriah. Sacrifice Him there as a burnt offering on a mountain I will show you." (Genesis 22:2 NIV)

Abraham does what God asks him to do. He loads up a donkey, tells his son that they will sacrifice to God, and head out. While they are traveling, Isaac asks his father where they will get the sacrifice, and Abraham's response is, "God himself will provide the lamb for the burnt offering, my son." They complete the journey. Abraham binds his son and raises the knife to kill his son, and God stops him. God tells him, "Do not lay a hand on the boy. Do not do anything to him. Now I know that you fear God because you have not withheld from me your son, your only son" (Genesis 22:12). Then God provided a ram for Abraham to sacrifice. Abraham called that place Jehovah-Jireh—the Lord will provide.

I love this story for many reasons, but the essential part is Abraham's trust that God would provide, which is a big deal because that wasn't always the case for Abraham. In other stories, he failed when it came to trusting God's provision. Abraham had another son named Ishmael, born from an adulterous relationship because Abraham didn't trust that God would provide him with a son the right way. He also lied about who his wife was so that he would be safe. But here, in this story, we see Abraham can fully trust God that he will provide what Abraham needs. I wonder what the story was like on the walk home. I can't imagine Isaac was feeling very good about how close he came to death at the hands of his father.

The point here is this: Unless God is the builder of the house, all of the work is in vain. What does that look like, you ask? Let me introduce you to Nehemiah. Nehemiah's story is found in the Old Testament in the book Nehemiah. Now Nehemiah was alive during the time after exile for the Jewish people. It was not a good time. Nehemiah 1:3 states,

> Those who survived the exile and are back
> in the province are in great trouble and disgrace.
> The wall of Jerusalem is broken down, and its
> gates have been burned with fire.

It was not a good camp. After Nehemiah heard the news, he became distraught, and he wept for days. Then he prayed. Nehemiah prayed because someone needed to fix his home city, and Nehemiah was sure it needed to be him. Nehemiah prayed that God would grant him favor to the king. Nehemiah approached the king and asked for everything he would need to accomplish the task at hand. The king said yes.

Nehemiah then went to work. He had a lot to do; he had to rally the people, gather materials, and lead a defeated nation. It was not easy; the city was attacked, people in the town didn't want to work, and some people balked at Nehemiah's leadership. The nation dealt with hunger, ridicule, and so much exhaustion. All of the negative influences did not deter Nehemiah. Why? Because he knew that the Lord was behind his actions. The Lord would provide all the necessary needs to accomplish the task.

Nehemiah was able to rebuild the wall and the gates in fifty-two days. The celebration that occurred was grand. It was not a party to honor Nehemiah though. It was a party that praised the Lord. The Bible says that they celebrated by reading the Law of God every day. Every day Ezra would get up and read out loud the Law of God. Nehemiah did more than rebuild a wall. He rebuilt a nation by turning them back toward God. This story may not be a home specifically, but the idea is the same—Nehemiah doesn't take the credit nor does he get the credit. The credit is God's and God's alone.

What can I do?

So many good Christian men have fallen into the trap that they are the provider of their homes. The role of provider has never been man's role. That role has always been God's. In many ways, the world has diminished God's role simply because it doesn't understand it. How about you? Are you stressed beyond belief? Do you wish that you could have a break? I challenge you to look at this simple verse. It doesn't say not to work hard or do your best, but it says that the builders labor in vain unless the Lord builds the house. If you don't trust the God of all creation with your home and house, all of your labor will seem lost. It will appear as though you will never see the end of the work or the struggle. Your assumptions will be correct. The work and labor will never end. I believe this is a part of the curse of Adam and Eve's sin. If you are working for the master builder, then the work is not in vain, the work will be blessed, and your house will be healthy and provided for just as God wants it.

Let me take you back to the good camp from earlier. You see, Tom went back and did all the work of building that camp, and Jim and I enjoyed that camp's benefits. I think we can see the same thing in our lives. God is always working. If we get out of the way and allow him to do the work, God will provide more than we ever really need; and when we do that, worry will begin to fade as we allow him to do the building. Just like it says in Matthew 6:25–34 (NIV),

> Therefore I tell you, do not worry about your life, what you will eat or drink; or about your body, what you will wear. Is not life more than food, and the body more than clothes? Look at the birds of the air; they do not sow or reap or store away in barns, and yet your heavenly Father feeds them. Are you not much more valuable than they? Can any one of you by worrying add a single hour to your life? And why do you worry about clothes? See how the flowers of the field grow. They do not labor or spin. Yet I tell you that not even Solomon in all his splendor was dressed like one of these. If that is how God clothes the grass of the field, which is here today and tomorrow is thrown into the fire, will he not much more clothe you—you of little faith? So do not worry, saying, "What shall we eat?" or "What shall we drink?" or "What shall we wear?" For the pagans run after all these things, and your heavenly Father knows that you need them. But seek first his kingdom and his righteousness, and all these things will be given to you as well. Therefore do not worry about tomorrow, for tomorrow will worry about itself. Each day has enough trouble of its own.

Chapter 3

Too Close for Comfort

Unless the Lord watches over the city, the
guards stand watch in vain.

—Psalm 127:1b

It had been a challenging hunt to this point. Since Phil had gone home the afternoon before, I was on my own today. The hike up the mountain had already really worn me out, but there were bulls up there, and I knew I needed to get up and get moving. It was already almost 7:00 a.m., so the chances of beating the bulls to the top had long gone, and they would be in their beds well before I got to the top. I pulled myself out of the sleeping bag, got dressed, and decided today I would get up top, do some exploring, and enjoy the day even if I didn't get an elk.

I started my ascent to the top. I took my time, found shady spots to rest, and worked my way up that massive climb. I had found this place through some good research with the game and fish department. The local biologist told me that this place was isolated and hard to get to, but there would be many elk and very few hunters. The two days before this one showed that his advice was valuable. We had seen a ton of elk and hadn't seen any other hunters. What he didn't say was that the way to this location was a grueling, almost vertical climb. No matter how slow I went or how often I would switch back, it was tough. This morning, though, I was moving slow—so slow, in fact, I knew that the day would be a waste for hunting.

After about an hour-and-a-half climb, I finally reached the top. I had worked up a pretty good sweat and decided to take off my shirts, air them out, and spray them down with some scent blocker, which would also give me some time to cool off. I found some branches to hang my shirt on and a log where I could sit. It was a lovely day. The cool breeze was working, and my body was cooling off nicely. I sat there, enjoying the quiet repose of the moment, feeling the draft and just relaxing. I reached into my backpack and pulled out my favorite hunting snack, the trusty crunchy granola bar, and a drink. I was comfortable, cool, and relaxed. It was a wonderful moment.

It occurred to me that the hike up this morning didn't seem as hard as the other two days. The last little bit almost seemed easy; also, I hadn't experienced any loose shale slides or had to fight any thick brush. I realized that how I had come up was the way to get up here the rest of my hunt, and even more importantly, this was the spot to begin my descent at the end of the day. I grabbed my GPS unit, made this spot a waypoint, and started to name the location "Down." It sounded like a good name since it was what I was going to use it for—how to get down the mountain later.

As I started to type in the word, a bull let out a bugle so close the hair on the back of my neck stood up. Here I was, GPS in hand, shirts off, and there was a bull very close. I saved the waypoint. It is still called "D10" today because I never remembered to go back and finish typing in the name. I quickly put my shirts back on, grabbed all my gear, and started in the direction I heard the bugle. It didn't take long before I was on the trail of this bull; he had bugled from the north-facing slope of a steep dark canyon, and man, was it pretty. The wind was in my face, and I could smell that the bull was close; but it was thick, so I couldn't see him. I would move very slow, cow call, and then listen. On my third cow call, I heard him again; this time, though, he didn't bugle. He thrashed a tree and grunted. I moved ever so closer, hoping to get a glimpse of this bull. I imagined me sneaking up, pulling the bow back, and sending the arrow deep into his chest. He would stop raking, and I would softly cow call.

When he was raking, I would move. Then, he suddenly stopped. I could hear him breathing, but I never could see him.

I heard a twig break to my left about that time, so I jerked my head around and saw something moving about one hundred yards away at the bottom of the canyon. I thought, *Yes, there is another bull, and he is coming this way.* I settled down in a shooting position, waiting for him to turn. I had only been able to see the movement until he cleared the trees. The animal was not an elk; instead, it was a giant black bear, and he was coming right at me. He was headed right to the spot I had last cow called. I sat there frozen, thinking a few thoughts: *1. Why didn't I buy that bear tag? 2. I don't have a sidearm (I never do; I just don't like them). 3. I need to get him away quietly so I can go after that bull. 4. Please don't attack me!*

It was a perfect situation: the wind was at my face, and I was quiet except for the fact that I could hear my heart beating. That bear came straight up the canyon, went right to where I last cow called, and stopped. He was maybe two feet away from me. I don't care how small you say black bears are; this one was huge. I could tell he didn't even know I was there. He stopped, sniffed the air, then stood up on his hind legs and took two long sniffs of the air. I was so frozen. There was an incredible sense of both excitement and a healthy sense of fear. In my mind, I kept thinking that if I had to, I would at least be able to stab this guy with an arrow as he was eating my face off. After he took his two big sniffs, he dropped back down to all fours. He was so close, and I felt the earth shake from his weight. He then turned around and went right back down the canyon, following the same trail. I sat there, completely stunned, shocked, and happy to be alive. I had almost forgotten what I had been doing in this canyon in the first place.

So, you ask, what does this story have to do with Psalm 127? Simple, really. I was defenseless against this bear. I had a weapon, sure, but in the end, had that bear attacked me, I likely wouldn't be here today. Maybe the attack doesn't immediately kill me, but how would I have crawled back down the several miles to camp, get in my vehicle, and get to help before I bled to death. Would I be able to crawl? I think in the end, I was at the mercy of whatever that bear decided to do, and I was under the protection of an almighty God who created that bear, saw that situation, and knew exactly how it would go. I had no control over that situation once I decided to sit and wait. I don't want to get into a sovereignty-of-God discussion here, but I think it is important to note that many, if not all, aspects of our lives are out of our control. We might be able to make decisions that seem safe and control your situation to a certain extent, but in the end, we don't control anything. Control is always an illusion. I can think of so many stories where this is repeatedly proven in my life, in others' lives, and in the Bible. One of my favorites from the Bible is the story of Gideon found in Judges 6 and 7.

Gideon's story

Let me introduce you to Gideon. We don't know a lot about Gideon; we know who his father is, we know when Gideon was alive, we know he was an Israelite, and we know he was from Manasseh.

The Israelites were in a pretty bad state. The Bible says in Judges 6:1–12,

> The Israelites did evil in the eyes of the Lord, and for seven years he gave them into the hands of the Midianites. Because the power of Midian was so oppressive, the Israelites prepared shelters for themselves in mountain clefts, caves and strongholds. Whenever the Israelites planted their crops, the Midianites, Amalekites and other eastern peoples invaded the country. They camped on the land and ruined the crops all the way to Gaza and did not spare a living thing for Israel, neither sheep nor cattle nor donkeys. They came up with their livestock and their tents like swarms of locusts. It was impossible to count them or their camels; they invaded the land to ravage it. Midian so impoverished the Israelites that they cried out to the Lord for help.

When the Israelites cried out to the Lord because of Midian, He sent them a prophet, who said, "This is what the Lord, the God of Israel, says: I brought you up out of Egypt, out of the land of slavery. I rescued you from the hand of the Egyptians. And I delivered you from the hand of all your oppressors; I drove them out before you and gave you their land. I said to you, 'I am the Lord your God; do not worship the gods of the Amorites, in whose land you live.' But you have not listened to me."

The angel of the Lord came and sat down under the oak in Ophrah that belonged to Joash the Abiezrite, where his son Gideon was threshing wheat in a winepress to keep it from the Midianites. When the angel of the Lord appeared to Gideon, he said, "The Lord is with you, mighty warrior."

Gideon is doing the same thing everyone else is doing—hiding—and he is not impressed by the angel of the Lord's greeting. The very first thing he does is question the angel about the Lord. Gideon says, "How can the Lord be with us? He has abandoned us."

The angel is not deterred. He tells Gideon that he will be the one to save the Israelites out of Midian's hand. The following few passages deal with Gideon trying to get out of this task. He claims that he and his family are weak, then he wants the Lord to give him a sign or two or three.

He is so afraid that he even built an altar to the Lord at night so people wouldn't see him doing it. After the Lord answers all his doubts, Gideon proceeded. Here is where the story gets good.

Gideon must have been convincing as well because he established a powerful camp of 32,000 men. Let me stop right here. This story, to me, illustrates how we work as Christians. Gideon doubts God, but once God establishes himself, we then go about using our strength to get the job done. God had different plans for Gideon, and what happens next is exactly the kind of thing God can do. God tells Gideon, "You have too many men for *me* to deliver Midian into their hands."

So God tells Gideon what to do to eliminate some men, and twenty-two thousand men left. Two-thirds of the army leaves, but God is not done. He tells Gideon that he still has too many. A test ensues, releasing another 21,700 men, leaving Gideon with only three hundred men. Gideon continues to follow God's instructions and defeats the Midianites with only three hundred men. Gideon obeyed God and led the Israelites for another forty years, and Israel saw great success. Why? Because he fully believed that God was the protector, and Israel followed God.

World's protection

I could go on and on about God's protection in my life or the life of others or in the Bible, but the fact is I believe that the Christians, in general, do not think that God protects, and neither do I. I believe it in theory, but I struggle with it in practice. Many of us can share a story of how something happened, and it just doesn't make sense how we are still alive. Something, though, gets in the way of us fully trusting God to protect us. I don't just mean protecting us from harm either.

The insurance industry in America in 2019 wrote 1.32 million dollars in premiums. I am not against insurance; it is a necessary evil in the world. I just want to point out that we might be too dependent on it. I don't know for sure. When I talk to people about their future, I know that it very rarely hinges on God's provision and protection but, instead, about their 401k, IRA, and life insurance. Why is this the case when over and over again we can see that God protects his people? Simple—we have experienced a plentiful level of protection from anyone but God.

We live in a world where we are protected from everything. Before I go any further, let me explain that I think all of these protections are good. I love and appreciate all the protections. Our cars have a plethora of safety features—ABS, airbags, backup cameras, safety braking features, dynamic cruise control, lane departure warning systems, and in some cases, cars that drive themselves. I even drove a car once that flashed a coffee cup at me and told me I should take a break from driving for a bit. Our homes are built to last, depending on which area of the US you live in, to withstand certain natural disasters. We stay connected to the people we love through our cell phones and track where family is at almost any time. The point is, we are protected more than we ever have been. Where does that leave God? The same place, as always, but not in our minds.

Through culture, through family and the church, I was taught that the husband's job is to be provider and protector. The idea of being provider and protector is not entirely a bad idea. I believe that the role of a man is to love his wife and his children, and I think that means we care for them and protect them from harm if we can—not that we always can. Tamra drives seventeen miles to work every day, works in a public school, and I am not there. My oldest daughter lives by herself, goes everywhere herself. My second oldest is married but lives eight hundred miles away, and my seventeen-year-old drives to school, work, and various other places all by herself. How in the world can I protect them? I can't. I checked online, and nobody sells protection bubbles to wrap my family in. The one true God protects them. But regardless, I was raised with the idea that it was my job. Television shows often showed men being the heroes or protectors of their families as well. This thought of the man protecting his woman was something that permeated my thoughts when I was younger.

God's protection

I took my family camping one year at one of my favorite lakes. We had rented a rustic cabin for a few days, towed a friend's boat up to the lake, and were ready to enjoy a great time with the family. When we arrived, we surveyed the cabin and started sharing how we were going to situate everyone. After that, we started the process of unpacking. Our oldest daughter, Harmony, was given the task of opening all the windows to allow the cool mountain air into the cabin. As we were unloading, we heard the bloodcurdling scream of

"*Phoebe!*" from the other room and a lot of yelling. Harmony was running out of the house, saying Phoebe had fallen out of a window. I was quick to get over to where the window was. There was Phoebe, sitting on the ground, crying and shaking. I assessed the situation, asked her some questions, and picked her up carefully to feel for damage. There was none; she was okay. She had fallen out of a window that was eight feet high and landed on her rear. Somehow, she had flipped over. Upon later inspection, she had missed two slabs of cement post footings by approximately six inches each. Why do I say this? Only God could protect her, and he did.

God's protection is far more than our earthly physical lives. Many of us know people who have passed away suddenly before their time. Maybe you say that God did not protect them. I have good news—God protects us in death. When he sent Jesus to die on the cross and forgive us of our sins, he accomplished the greatest protection of all. I think what I am trying to get here is this: *You cannot* protect your family. No man is strong enough, fast enough, or present enough to accomplish that task. We must depend entirely on God to protect our families and friends.

Depending on God might be hard to do. I will be the first to admit that even though I trust God, it is not always easy. I want everything to be okay, I want my family to be happy, and I will do anything to accomplish those tasks; the problem is I can't do it. Tamra reminds me when I get like that that it is the Lord who protects us unless the Lord guards the city. My mom used to say, "I brought you into this world. I can take you out!" Of course, she was joking, but there is a truth in that statement. God created everything, and that includes each one of us. He is the author of life, and he will protect that life as he sees fit. One of my favorite passages that illustrate this is found in Isaiah 41:

> "So do not fear, for I am with you; do not
> be dismayed, for I am your God. I will strengthen
> you and help you; I will uphold you with my
> righteous right hand. All who rage against you
> will surely be ashamed and disgraced; those

who oppose you will be as nothing and perish. Though you search for your enemies, you will not find them. Those who wage war against you will be as nothing at all.

"For I am the Lord your God who takes hold of your right hand and says to you, 'Do not fear; I will help you. Do not be afraid, you worm Jacob, little Israel, do not fear, for I myself will help you,'" declares the Lord, your Redeemer, the Holy One of Israel.

"See, I will make you into a threshing sledge, new and sharp, with many teeth. You will thresh the mountains and crush them, and reduce the hills to chaff. You will winnow them, the wind will pick them up, and a gale will blow them away. But you will rejoice in the Lord and glory in the Holy One of Israel.

"The poor and needy search for water, but there is none; their tongues are parched with thirst. But I the Lord will answer them; I, the God of Israel, will not forsake them. I will make rivers flow on barren heights, and springs within the valleys. I will turn the desert into pools of water, and the parched ground into springs.

"I will put in the desert the cedar and the acacia, the myrtle and the olive. I will set junipers in the wasteland, the fir and the cypress together, so that people may see and know, may consider and understand, that the hand of the Lord has done this, that the Holy One of Israel has created it."

God will protect, but we have to allow it. His protection may not always look the way we will like it. I am sorry to say that loved ones will die, tragedies will occur, stock markets will crash, and fortunes will crumble. God, though, will last forever, and he knows everything you need. He knows all your fears and all your worries. You can lay them to rest because it is not your job to protect the things you love. Jesus says in Matthew 11:28–30,

> Come to me, all you who are weary and burdened, and I will give you rest. Take my yoke upon you and learn from me, for I am gentle and humble in heart, and you will find rest for your souls. For my yoke is easy and my burden is light.

Stop trying to take the job of protector away from God, and let him do what only he can do.

Chapter 4

Forced Rest

In vain, you rise early and stay up late, toiling for food
to eat—for he grants sleep to those he loves.
—Psalm 127:2

Waking up at 4:00 a.m. was challenging, to say the least. I had been working very long hours the whole year. Earlier in the year, the current senior pastor decided to move on, and the deacons asked me to come on as interim senior pastor. They offered a small stipend for the job, so I gladly took it. With three children and another one on the way, it seemed like a good idea. I had also started my online graduate program and was still in charge of all other aspects of the church ministry. I had torn my Achilles tendon in January and had spent three months on crutches.

For a while, I couldn't even drive. I relied entirely on others to get me from point A to point B, take care of the kids, and deal with a lot of pain—not from the Achilles but the shoulder injuries ensued from the crutches. I was in terrible shape. I was angry all the time, thought terrible thoughts, and knew I wasn't right. I was pretty sure I was dealing with depression, but I hid it well due to my ability to move forward without too much hassle. I was struggling through a lot of things and did not have time to deal with them—but I had been looking forward to this hunt; it was something I just *needed*. I felt like a good hunt would fix the doldrums.

We had left pretty late in the afternoon the day before and got up to camp; we took our time to set up camp. It was an excellent camp, one that would suffice for the next four days. I was not hunting this time. I was helping. I was helping one of my best friends, Tom, on his elk hunt. I was very excited. It had been ten months since my surgery, and I was off crutches, out of the boot, and ready to test out my new Achilles. It still hurt quite a bit, but I hadn't done anything to put it to the test. That night we sat around and talked and enjoyed each other's company. We even had a campfire, which we didn't do on our archery hunts, but Tom was hunting with a muzzleloader this year, so it seemed like something we could do. We stayed up for a while and went to bed, ready for a restful night so we would be up ready for the hike in the morning.

What we didn't know was that we had camped next to the local town's favorite teenager hangout on a Friday night, so about midnight, the meadow below us came "alive." I was awakened by the sound of glass packs, loud music, and a lot of hollering. It was not the sound I wanted, but it was the sound that I was given. I did not sleep very much, and so, going back to the beginning, waking up at 4:00 a.m. was difficult, but it is what we did.

We had scouted the area pretty hard, and the walk was uphill about two miles, then we would continue our hike into some pretty neat country. Of course, the hope was we would run into elk once we got to the top. It was a challenging hike; going uphill in the dark always has its difficulties especially with a newly repaired Achilles tendon. We would stop a lot and look behind us. During one of these stops, my friend Allen and I got into a little bit of an argument. He was sure that people were right behind us and we needed to go faster. At one point, he saw some lights. I don't remember all the details, but it is one of my favorite hunting memories to this day. We got to the top and were pleased to see we were the only ones there.

Allen and I were the callers, Jim was the cameraman, and Tom was the hunter. So Allen and I started calling to see if we could get anything going. It was not going the way we wanted; we would call and be greeted with silence. During this time in my hunting journey, I was a firm believer in calling and calling a lot, and I still am; it is just fun. So we continued our calling sequences. We were both getting pretty discouraged. We would ask Tom where he wanted to go since he was the hunter, and we would go that way. Once we got up top, it was clear there was a lot of territory to cover on foot; and when you are an elk hunter, the other factor that comes into play is, "Would I want to pack an elk out of here?" So we took our time and continued calling, walking, and calling again. Then, when we were least expecting it, which happens a lot when hunting, a bull answered back.

Allen and I found a log to hide behind and told Tom and Jim to go set up. What happened next might be one of my favorite calling experiences ever. Allen and I crouched behind a log. We had put up a decoy in front of us, so it was hard for him and me to see the action, but the excitement became quite high. Every time the bull bugled closer, Allen and I would look at each other and smile: "He is coming." It took a little bit, but then suddenly there he was, about one hundred yards out, on top of the hill, under a ponderosa pine. And then he bugled, grunted, and peed on himself. It was awesome! Allen and I continued calling and kept waiting for Tom to shoot, but it just wasn't happening. The bull walked right over to where Jim and Tom were set up. Finally, Tom shot. He told us later that he had to freeze because the bull was feet away. After the shot, the bull went back to the ponderosa tree, where he took his last breath.

The celebration that took place after was grand. It was a celebration for the books. Tom had succeeded in harvesting his elk, and we had it all on camera. It was cool. The work began now, and it wasn't until I saw the video that I noticed the amount I was limping. We sent Allen and Jim back to the trucks to get the pack, and Tom and I got to work on field, dressing the elk. Before we got all that going, though, we took a moment and rested. It was an excellent rest, one that we had earned and required, because the work ahead would be challenging but worth it. We were able to pack the elk out and get down to the trucks at about noon.

Here is where I got weird. We would go to town, drop the elk off at the processors, and come back to camp and relax for a few days, but I wasn't feeling it. As I said, I had been struggling, and this was a situation where I felt like just going back home. Plus, it would mean that Tamra was not taking care of the kids alone. So I went home and stayed there while the guys went back to camp.

Not long after this trip, Tamra insisted I see my doctor and talk about what was happening. She was worried for me. She was probably worried for us. As I look back at that time in our lives, I am so glad that Tamra was strong; she knew what I needed to do and made sure I did it. I wasn't myself anymore and would snap at the drop of a hat. I went to see my doctor, and he immediately diagnosed me with depression and sent me home with a sample pack of the medicine and a prescription to take.

I won't mention the medicine's name because I don't remember it, but it worked. I remember feeling a sense of calmness come over me, and when I would lie down, I would sleep—like really sleep. I remember thinking that if Tamra came in, told me she sold my truck, and bought me a small car, I would have been like, "Coo." I took this medicine for a couple of weeks and got some much-needed rest. I had forgotten what it meant to rest.

The world's rest

I, like many people, get busy. As I said earlier, I am part of a family of very hard workers and, in many ways, was told if you don't work, you don't eat. Being a hard worker is biblical; several verses deal with this topic:

- Proverbs 21:25: "The craving of a sluggard will be the death of him, because his hands refuse to work."
- 1 Timothy 5:8: "Anyone who does not provide for their relatives, and especially for their own household, has denied the faith and is worse than an unbeliever."
- Proverbs 14:23: "All hard work brings a profit, but mere talk leads only to poverty."

Although we are told to be hard workers, the problem exists when we work for the wrong reasons. Let me share some verses about *why* we are supposed to work:

- 1 Corinthians 10:31: "So whether you eat or drink or whatever you do, do it all for the glory of God."
- Colossians 3:17: "And whatever you do, whether in word or deed, do it all in the name of the Lord Jesus, giving thanks to God the Father through him."
- 1 Corinthians 3:9: "For we are co-workers in God's service; you are God's field, God's building."

I just wanted to be clear about some things before I work this passage with you—since this is a bit of a transition verse, I will refer back to some of the earlier verses. After reading this verse repeatedly, I feel that this may be the most important verse of the passage.

I had gotten so busy with all of my jobs and tasks that I could no longer rest. I believe it is a problem of our culture. I decided to look at the ways we rest and see if the average American is even resting. So after surfing the web, I have found this—the average amount of sleep per person is now less than six hours a night. The average American has about sixteen days of vacation time given to them. Still the average American vacation is just over four days, and the average American works 8.8 hours a day.

Add to the work days the amount of pressure we, as parents, are put under to have our children involved in multiple sports and activities, making sure our children get into the rights colleges and schools, making sure our children experience all that the world has to offer, and we can see how rest is hard to come by. Yet I think that more than not, people long for rest, long for a good night's sleep, me included. Maybe this is easier than we think; maybe not.

I have ADD. I mean it. I can hardly walk around without fidgeting with something, let alone sit still. The clicking of a pen almost always accompanies our staff meetings here at church. I sometimes feel sorry for those around me with my noises and movements. I think it is one of the reasons I don't sleep very long into the morning.

For as long as I remember, I wake at 5:00 a.m. or earlier. I even wear it like a badge. Whether it is healthy or not, I don't know, but it is my life. I am terrible at just sitting and doing nothing. I think it is one of the reasons I like hunting—the movement, the constant job of looking and finding, even when sitting still; but there have been moments of rest that have gone beyond, and they have always been forced.

Let me refocus you on this verse:

> In vain you rise early and stay up late, toiling for food to eat—for he grants sleep to those he loves.

So how does this verse fit within this culture? It doesn't. Let me tell you why. As a culture, we do not depend on God. I am going to generalize here because I feel like I addressed this when talking about verse 1.

But God is no longer the provider. God is no longer the protector. We provide by working hard, and we teach our children that hard work will reward them with good things, and we exhibit that what we get with hard work is stuff. We are driven by stuff. Let me take a moment to tell you that I am at least one poster child for this. I don't know if my family didn't have a lot or if it is just my sinful nature, but I like stuff. I like nice stuff. I don't own many nice things due to the nature of being a pastor with six children, but I still like it and want it. I look at vehicles online on average of fifteen minutes a day—that's right, every day. I don't know that it consumes me, but it is far too often. I think about different things all the time—another house, a new travel trailer, a new truck, and even a new job. I don't think about a new wife (I don't just put that in here to make Tamra happy; it is true). So I guess I tell you that so you understand that I feel the struggle, and I have worked hard to get where I am today even if it isn't where I expected to be.

The drive for more surrounds us. I enjoy movies and series. I love watching the TV, the computer, the phone screen, or even the screen at the gas station. I can watch stuff a lot. One thing I notice is that they all advertise more and better—dating sites, job sites, car sites, and even explaining why the gas I am putting into my car is better than the stations down the road. It is a bombardment in my life, and there is nowhere I can go to get away from the better things. I was listening to the radio a couple of days ago, and an ad came on for this new type of job that anyone can do, and they could make six figures their first year. I remember thinking, *I could do that.* The truth is even in the church world, we are bombarded by things that claim to be better, will do more for a lower cost.

As I am sitting here, writing, I think, *I should be upset by the amount of advertising I am subject to.* I know better though—I don't *have* to look at screens. My point is the drive for more is real, and with that drive comes vanity. What is the world pushing? Vanity. You can make more, have more, and be more. I can't get mad at the world, but I can at least begin to see how the world is vying for my attention and taking me away from some important things, and one of those things is rest.

In all its wisdom, the world praises the hard workers, the people who are making it. I love sports, and some athletes do more than others. If they are successful, we tout their achievements and say, "Look at him. They are the best. Every other athlete should use them as a model." So athletes start to get up earlier, eat different foods, watch more films—all in the hopes of becoming that athlete.

Parents will do this to their children. I have six children, and so far, they are all pretty decent athletes. I have tried not to push my children into doing more than they wanted, but I don't want them to be sloths. We are often asked to join travel teams, which play outside the season, usually a little more competition and always more money. There is always this idea that it will make them better, making them more apt to be picked up by a college. The travel team dream can be pretty tempting; however, my wife and I are cautious. For us, athletics is not a ticket item; it should be fun.

I will share how this plays out in my son's life. My son, Nehemiah, might be one of the fastest kids I have ever seen, I love watching him run, and he loves running. Because of his speed, coaches love to drool over him like he is some great athlete. He is athletic, built like an athlete, and has no idea just how many people wish they were blessed with his natural abilities. The truth is sports don't drive him. I believe that sports are good for a child's character, so I force my kids to at least play them. There are no expectations—just have fun. However, the pressure that we have received to get him on to a travel team for baseball has been pretty high, but he doesn't want to do it. Even if he did, I want him to do what he enjoys even if I don't understand it. Our goal has to be for him to love life and live it to the fullest in Christ. If sports does that, we will talk; but if it doesn't, we will find what does. My concern is that many parents are working too hard to ensure that their kids are the *best* at everything, so they rise early and stay up late in vain. The goal for our kids and us must be that we focus on God, not ourselves. My point here is don't be so wrapped up in success that you can't see God.

In seeing God, trusting God, and being willing to give God the glory that we will live this life correctly. The start of the verse says "in vain," so the problem isn't getting up early or staying up late. It is "in vain." If our goal in rising early and staying up late is for the sake of our good and our glory, then we will not have the ultimate success. I feel like I am beating a dead horse here, so let me sum up these two essential ideas: Work is necessary, and good workers are biblical, but if the work and the worker are only doing it for the sake of "food to eat" or things, then they are doing the work in vain because it will only satisfy their needs and desires. A life like this will mean that rest might be hard to come by the rest needed to keep going at that pace.

God grants sleep

Let's turn to our last little section here, which is this: "God grants sleep to those he loves." When was the last time you had a perfect sleep? You know the one I am talking about—that kind of sleep where you can't even remember when you went to sleep but you wake up refreshed and ready to go. You know what I am talking about, right? For me, I think I had that sleep over twenty-seven years ago before our first child was born. That isn't true, but those types of restful nights are not often. I wonder why. I think there are many factors to it that I think get in the way. I live a sedentary life; I don't work outside all day tilling the ground or anything like that, so my body is never really that tired. I think this is one of the reasons I like hunting. It does get me out for days hiking and moving and does exhaust the body. Most of my life is spent at my computer or in my truck. I recently got a standing desk—even the fact that I say that is pretty funny. Anyway, because my life is sedentary, I tend not to be physically tired at bedtime. The second factor is the fact that the world and our electronics never sleep. We are forever plugged in—so much so that our devices now tray and tell us to turn them off. There are also the factors that I will focus on here in the following few paragraphs, which I think are the most important, and that is our mental health and those associated with it.

When it comes to sleep, we depend on our feelings, stress levels, relationships, and stuff. Yet here in Psalm 127, we are told *God* grants sleep to those he loves. So if we depend on God for our provision and on God for our protection, then why wouldn't we depend on God for our sleep? Even this seems like an interesting concept to me as I sit here and write it: Depend on God for our rest. What does that look like? What does that mean? How does that work? Let me take some time to answer these questions as best I can.

Before I talk about that, let me tell you another one of my favorite Bible stories. This one is from the New Testament. In Mark 4, we read a story of Jesus spending a hectic day teaching at the lake. There were so many people there that he asked the disciples to have a boat ready so the people would not crowd him. People with diseases pushed forward to be healed, and people with demons were falling at his feet, calling out his name. The crowd was so large that he went up on the mountainside. It was a chaotic day. When the end of the day arrived, Jesus said, "Let us go to the other side." They left the crowd behind, and this is where it gets interesting. Just in case you ever wondered if Jesus got tired, here is your proof.

A furious squall came up, and those in the boats were frightened, but Jesus was asleep on a cushion at the stern of the ship. The men woke Jesus up and said, "Don't you care about us?" Jesus wakes up and calms the storm. But I can only imagine how deep the sleep was that Jesus didn't even wake up until he was shaken by one of the men. I love it; Jesus wakes up, calms the storm, and then rebukes his disciples. The story reminds of the times that one of the children came in and woke me up because they were scared. I asked, "What are you afraid of?" Then I prayed with them and went back to sleep. The Bible doesn't say it, but I think Jesus said what he said and lay back down to go to sleep. I bet the disciples were a little less likely to wake him up after that. Jesus knew the importance of sleep, and it sounds like he was able to sleep pretty soundly.

God created rest. Therefore, he can give it when necessary. So here are my humble thoughts on sleep: Make sure you stay on a schedule as best you can. God scheduled his rest. It says that God took the seventh day and rested. It was a part of his plan from the beginning. It should be a part of our daily routine. Plan it. Plan what time you go to bed and plan what time you get up and stick to it. There will be moments, even seasons of life where it might be difficult, but try as hard as you can to stick to the plan. If God thought it was essential to plan, so should we. My goal is I go to bed by 10:30 every night and wake up at 5:30 every morning. I wouldn't expect everyone to have my plan, but try and stick to whatever your plan is. Ask God to bless your plan for sleep. If you have young children, pray they will allow you to adhere to the program. If you have adult children, pray they will let you stick to your plan. When you establish the plan, stick to it, and let God do the rest.

Some people have tough times sleeping, and I don't want to be remiss and not speak to those times. In my life, I have found that outside of new babies, significant life changes, or special events, the things that made it hard for me to sleep were worries. The Bible has a lot to say about anxiety. Philippians 4:6–7 is probably the most used verse here. It says,

> Do not be anxious about anything, but in every situation, by prayer and petition, with thanksgiving, present your requests to God. And the peace of God, which transcends all understanding, will guard your hearts and your minds in Christ Jesus.

Another verse that speaks to this is found in Matthew 6:25:

> Therefore I tell you, do not worry about your life, what you will eat or drink; or about your body, what you will wear. Is not life more than food, and the body more than clothes?

These two verses and many others help us know that worry and anxiety are not a part of the Christian walk, and those things will derail our sleep and rest. When I struggle with sleep because of worry, I pray.

I think the most important thing is to always—and I mean always—remember the last three words in this verse: "to those he loves." God loves you absolutely, without exception, no-strings-attached love. He takes great delight in loving you so much so that he sent his son to die on a cross for you. He grants you sleep, but you have to be willing to accept it, just like the gift of salvation. Worry and anxiety will rob you of that sleep.

One last thing. I am not a stranger to mental illness. I have multiple family members who struggle with mental illness. Sleep is something that those with mental illnesses struggle with. Please, please, please. Please make sure you seek medical care if you are having serious issues sleeping. I feel like that might go throughout the whole first part of this passage. Mental illness can cripple someone from being able to experience God's love, his provision, and his protection. I do not want anyone reading this to think that I am discounting what mental illness can do. Medical professionals have access to medicines that could help the brain chemistry so that you can see clearly.

Chapter 5

Part 1: Conclusion

It might be easier than you think

When I was thirteen years old, my dad was living with my stepmom, Lorraine. Lorraine is from Brooklyn, New York, and she is a trooper. Let me take a moment to let you meet Lorraine. Do you know the stories of stepmoms like the one in Cinderella? That is not Lorraine. Lorraine was and still is a fantastic stepmom. She loved me through some tough years when she didn't have to. Lorraine taught me how to do laundry, keep a clean room, and care about people who were not like me. It is hard to explain how important she is to my life. She took me in and loved me when she didn't have to, and she is a part of the fabric of who I am. Lorraine had so much to do with what I believe about marriage roles because she thought differently than anyone else I had ever met.

Lorraine had decided to come hunting with us this year, and for whatever reason, Dad had decided to take her car on the trip, which, to my recollection, was a 1980 Chevy Nova. Interesting vehicle to take on a deer hunt, I know. We stayed at my grandpa's cabin in Lapine. We woke up early and started driving down the road pretty early. I don't remember the time. It was opening morning deer season, and this was Lorraine's first time ever hunting. I get the feeling that Dad had tried to talk Lorraine out of coming on that hunt by telling her hunting was hard. It would be long days walking up and down canyons and maybe not seeing any deer at all. But this day would be different.

So, here we were in Lorraine's brown Chevy Nova, traveling down a dirt logging road when Dad sees a deer on the side of the road. He gets out, goes to the edge of the road, and shoots. I was still in the car and remember seeing the biggest deer I had ever seen running away, so I thought Dad had missed him. Dad had not missed him and was pretty sure he had shot a little spike buck right off the bat on opening morning. I, of course, was very excited. I couldn't wait to get this animal back to camp and start the work of processing. We walked up to the deer. It was a beautiful four-by-four buck with a twenty-nine-inch spread, and Dad had shot him opening morning right off the road, driving a Chevy Nova. It was Dad's largest mule deer buck. Needless to say, Lorraine didn't believe Dad that this was so hard, and maybe it isn't.

There have been other hunts that have been easy as well. Many years later, after doing all the hard stuff for three days, I walked up a small canyon behind camp and shot a spike elk in less than fifteen minutes. The elk was less than fifty yards from the road and not even half a mile from camp. Hunting can be challenging; more times than not, it is difficult, but many hunters in the Western United States never scale large canyons or climb tall mountains and are successful. One year Dad and I had walked out of camp, maybe one hundred yards, and two small bucks walked right to us; and in less than five minutes, we had filled our tags. There was the deer that ran right in front of us when we parked the truck to go potty. The antelope that walked within two hundred yards of camp that my dad shot. I can go on and on about all of the times we have had hunts that made it look easy. The same is true in life. Whether it is building a home, protecting a family, or getting the rest we need, I sometimes wonder if we make it too hard. Maybe it's easier than we think.

Stay with me here. What if all the troubles of this world are simply *vanity*? Think about these first two verses and hear the words:

Unless the Lord builds the house,
the builders labor in vain.

Unless the Lord watches over the city,
the guards stand watch in vain.
In vain you rise early
and stay up late,
toiling for food to eat—
for He grants sleep to those he loves.

Three times we see the word *vain* used. The Hebrew word is *Shav*, which means "wasteful idolatry." Now I am melding together many different word studies to come up with that simple definition, but I think it fits. Look around. Look around at the vanity in our world, and it is easy to see how it is wasteful. Yet even believers fall into the trap of vanity. Why? Because we are all creatures that use our senses and our history to tell us what we lack. If I drive down the road and see a prettier or bigger house, I think that the person that owns that place must be more successful than me. If I see a gated community with many beautiful homes, I think those people might be safer than me, and if I see an ad for a bed that will guarantee me a good night's rest, I think maybe I need that bed.

Not only am I faced with the reality that many people in the world have more than me seem happier than me and have more fun than me, I also face it in the fake world—Facebook, Hollywood, commercials, and countless other social media sites that people use to express how fantastic life is. But it is all in vain. I don't want to beat everyone up here, but I want you to consider what drives us every day might be evil vanity. I believe that these first couple of verses hit the nail on the head (duh, it's the Bible). We do a lot of chasing the next thing because of our vanity. We are a people unsatisfied with what the God of the universe has given us, and we don't accept his goodness, his protection, or his rest.

What if instead of chasing after the next best thing, we asked God to provide for us everything we need, nothing else, and were satisfied with that? Let that linger. Look around at all of your belongings; look at your monthly subscriptions. Could you live with less? Could you? I guarantee you could. I know that I could. I enjoy the many things that the world offers, and I too chase the newer and better. I have lived in Roswell for seventeen years; in those seventeen years, I have owned eight different vehicles. Maybe that is not a lot for you, but I think it is a lot. I justify the constant change by saying I don't buy new vehicles; I buy well-used cars. But soon after I buy another car, I am online at the dealerships looking for my next good deal.

Of course, the following vehicle will have some unique features or accomplish some critical tasks that I can't do now. I might be right in line with many others, but in the end, I know that my constant searching is not godly. God can provide me far less, and I should be far happier. As a hunter, I find that the industry has sucked me in as well. I need to get further, with less work, have a better camp, and be able to sneak quieter, smell less, and can shoot the fly off a scorpion's back at one thousand yards. Back to my family—my grandpa hunted from a stump with a red crusher cap and wearing wool pants. I look at pictures of my grandparents when they were younger and realize our world has become far too accommodating, and our spiritual health has paid the price. So I ask again, Could you live with less? I guess the more important question is this: Can you be satisfied with what God has built for you? I believe this is easier than we make it, but we fight it because of our sinful nature.

The same is true in our need for protection. The amount of time, energy, and money we give to protecting our assets, our future, and our lives is quite extensive. If we consider the *why* we spend so much on protection, we may see that it is all in vain. What are we protecting? In the end, *our* stuff, *our* families, and *our* pride. Protecting these things can be a daunting task. I was looking just the other day at the security camera section at a store. (I remember when that wasn't even a thing.) I sat and looked at how many cameras one could buy, install, and monitor to protect their home and family. I thought to myself, *Why? Why is there a whole section dedicated to camera security? I just wanted some milk.* I couldn't just walk right past the area though; I stared at the many angles, the cost, the installation gear, and thought, *What is the reason? Vanity.*

You see, all of these cameras are focused on keeping stuff. Oh, without being mean, I guess you could say it is about protecting your family's safety. Still, I have a hard time with that, considering if someone decides to break into my house while we are all asleep, that individual will do damage before I can even get the cobwebs out of my head. I don't want you to think I live without protection or that we should be unwise. I lock my doors, I own an alarm that would be pretty loud if someone broke into our home while we were gone, and I have a doorbell with a camera. (Come on, those things are cool—I love to talk to my kids when they go outside and I am at work. That is just fun.) But it is important to understand that in the end, God protects. Our efforts to "guard the city" are useless because unless the Lord watches it, there is no absolute, true protection. It doesn't have to be that hard. Incredibly, our world has taught us to live in fear of those who will steal and rob our stuff but not live in fear of our souls. Jesus has something very pointed to say about that in Matthew 6:19–20:

> Do not store up for yourselves treasures on earth, where moths and vermin destroy, and where thieves break in and steal. But store up for yourselves treasures in heaven, where moths and vermin do not destroy, and where thieves do not break in and steal.

If we take this verse to heart, then and only then can we release the protection to God. I believe that this is not as hard as we make it. Still, once again, our sinful nature, like the world, has caused us to lose sight of what is truly important, and in the end, we become dependent on all the ways we are responsible for our protection when that falls entirely on God. It is easier than we think it is, but it will require a shift in thinking.

If we truly allow the Lord to build the house and the Lord to guard the city, we will find proper rest instead of toiling in vain. Think for a moment about the last time you didn't sleep well. What was the cause? Was it worry? Was it anxiety? Was it selfish ambition? I lose sleep when I worry. I have six children, so there are times that I stay awake wondering about their problems, their lives, their successes. This is sin. That is all. I will talk a lot more about the ultimate job we have with our children in the coming sections, but staying awake worrying about them is a sin. I'm sorry if that offends you. I don't think that it is our job to worry about them.

Back to my point. I have discussed lack of sleep with many people in my time, and I have noticed that someone will lose sleep over something they can't control most of the time. This verse summarizes this section well: "In vain, you rise early and stay up late." If *you* are the provider and protector, you better be the first person to work and the last person to leave. Our society encourages that behavior. Those who are hard workers get rewarded by the world—promotions, higher wages, better stuff—but what is the cost? I think that this verse sums it up by saying God grants sleep to those he loves. God created rest, he formed our bodies to sleep; and if we are chasing after vanity, we will lose it. The world teaches us "reach for the stars." God teaches us "reach for me." I want to be clear here; the Bible says we are to work, we should earn our way in this life, but we should not be working to boost our vanity. We should be working to glorify God.

Colossians 3:23 states,

> Whatever you do, work at it with all your heart, as working for the Lord, not for human masters.

Guess what—you can be your own human master. You can set the standard so high that you are not able to reach it. You will lose sleep. You will have an unhealthy family. You will not be joyful. Look at your life right now. Ask these questions. Be as honest as you can.

1. Who builds your house? Unless the Lord builds your house, you labor in vain.
2. Who protects your house? Unless the Lord watches over the city, the guards watch in vain.
3. How much sleep do you get? Unless the Lord builds, and unless the Lord protects, sleep is hard. However, if we trust him, he grants us sleep.

If we can give the responsibility of provision and protection to God, I believe that we will sleep better, be happier, and live better. I don't think it is as hard as it looks; it might just be too easy.

Chapter 6

Part 2: Children

Children are a heritage from the Lord, offspring a reward
from him. Like arrows in the hands of a warrior are
children born in one's youth. Blessed is the man whose
quiver is full of them. They will not be put to shame
when they contend with their opponents in court.
—Psalm 127:3–5

Labor day weekend came fast, and I had an archery elk tag burning
a hole in my pocket. I had already planned my trip, but I wanted
to go to some scouting and take my two daughters, Harmony and
Maryruth, with me, so we loaded up the truck and headed into the
woods early on that Saturday morning. I knew where I was going,
and we were well on our way when I heard a hissing coming from
my rear tire. Within a few moments, we were on the side of the dirt
road with a flat tire. I told the kids to go and play over by the creek as
Jim and I made short work of the tire situation. As we got under the
truck to remove the spare, we noticed a padlock that I did not have
the key for holding the spare tire on. (One of the issues with buying
well-used vehicles is that sometimes you don't get *all* the necessary
equipment.) We did not have bolt cutters, so we waited and hoped
someone would come by and maybe help us out. We were going to
be waiting. We stopped the first truck that came by (which happened

to take about an hour) and asked if they could give one of us a lift into town where we could get some bolt cutters.

Lo and behold, the guy had some in his truck, and we could get the tire changed. We piled back in the truck and headed to the spot where we would walk in. By now, the kids were hungry and had lost the initial excitement of the *hunt*. We got out of the truck, had lunch, let the kids play a little, and then decided to head up the mountain. It was a pretty good hike, but Harmony and Maryruth handled it like troopers; I think Harmony was eleven and Maryruth was seven. As we walked up the hill, two spike elk came down and got pretty close—not close enough for a shot but close enough that the kids became reenergized to see what was up top. We walked for a while and reached the top. There was plenty of sign, but it was the middle of the day, and it was pretty warm, so hunting became walking.

As we were walking, we came out into a beautiful bowl with a lovely meadow. We found a nice big tree and sat there in the shade, waiting before we headed back. We napped, and occasionally we would cow call just to see if anything would happen. Nothing did. It was very relaxing. Then out of the blue came an elk. It was a group of three small bulls, and they walked right down in front of us, the little spike less than five yards away. I wasn't shooting a spike, especially since it was opening day, but there was a little three-point that had walked down as well. We let the spike walk away, and I crawled to the spot where the three-point was. (Now, I am not the most athletic guy in the world, but I think I can handle my own. Trying to army crawl with a bow in hand is not easy, and I know Jim was laughing at me as well as Harmony and Maryruth. They told me so.) When I reached the spot where the three-point was, he was gone; but there was another bull there, a small forked horn. I decided I was not interested in shooting a small bull, so I snuck out and headed back to the group.

The kids had many questions as to why I didn't shoot the spike, why didn't I shoot the other bull. The kids were pretty upset. They wanted an animal on the ground. I explained why when the distinct smell of elk greeted us, and we knew there were more just across the meadow. We sat there for a while, hoping they would come down, but no luck. We talked for a little bit; then after much pleading from Harmony, we decided to go over and see what type of elk was in the trees. It was at this point that Harmony negotiated. She wanted me to shoot an elk so bad. She asked how big it would need to be for me to shoot it. I responded that if it were a three-point or better, I would shoot it. An agreement was made, and we were off. We got up to where we felt the elk might be and started sneaking on the trail—well, most of us. Maryruth was pretty done by this time, and although she was a trooper, she was rather fidgety. We walked down the trail when a small rag horn bull stood up less than twenty yards away broadside. He didn't even care that we were there. We were all frozen as he stared at us—all of us, that is except Maryruth, who was down on a knee. She had noticed something on her pants and smacking her leg, trying to get whatever it was off there. The elk had laser-focused on her location. I drew my bow back and had this bull in my sights, but something kept me from releasing the arrow. So many thoughts raced through my mind:

1. This was opening day, and I had seen six bulls. I wanted a bigger one, and if this was any indication of how my hunt would go, I should be able to get a bigger one.
2. It was late Saturday afternoon, and I had to work tomorrow. Shooting this bull in this location would mean a pretty substantial pack out, which would mean a very late night with the two girls.
3. What if I missed it? Did I even have the time to find this bull?

I let the bull walk away. The whole time it walked, it stared at Maryruth, who was smacking her leg. I don't even know if she saw the elk. Harmony was disappointed, and she let me know about it. When I went back for my trip with only adults, I did not see one bull, let alone one to shoot.

Even though I didn't shoot an elk that day, it was one of my favorite trips because those are memories that I will never forget. Maryruth and Harmony don't forget them either. These memories are so important to my family because children are a large part of my life. It is one of the reasons I work in children's ministry and one of the reasons that I wrote this book. It is also an important story because it provides yet another story where I see God providing when it didn't make sense. The idea that I saw that many elk when I was with my children vs. how many I saw without them is noteworthy.

I split this book into two parts because I believe that the passage allows for it. Before I move into that, let me assure you that I think the two sections, although very different, are very much playing off each other. Before we can raise or mentor children, it is vitally important that we have our priorities in order. Think about this for a second. How can we speak into the lives of children without first being in a right relationship with God? I am not talking about whether or not you have decided to follow Jesus. I am talking about whether or not you have decided to give him the rightful place in your life as provider and protector. If you haven't, children will be a drain to your very soul. Children are stinky, smelly, selfish little creatures. They typically don't listen very well, and they have a lot of nasty habits. Children drain your bank account quicker than a Las Vegas casino and need more attention than anything in this world. They will eat you out of house and home, they will argue with you, and they will yell at you. Without a doubt, raising children is the most challenging job you will ever have. However, it is also the most important, most rewarding, and greatest blessing you could be given. That, I believe, is the information. The concept of raising children is the center point here. Although there is not much said, the content of these verses is important. Let's get started.

Chapter 7

Proud Moments

Children are a heritage from the Lord.
                                                    —Psalm 127:3a

I don't remember my exact age. I am guessing I was fifteen or sixteen. It was deer season in Oregon, and we were hunting our favorite
unit. The area was a logging area, so there were a lot of roads. My
dad loved the area because the game and fish had gone through and
designated that only specific routes could have motor vehicles during
hunting season. The roads made it easier to hunt deer. You could
walk up and down these roads and be very quiet. You didn't have
to walk through the brush, you had a clear path, and no one would
drive past you, kick up dust, and scare the deer away. Another excellent advantage is that those who were road hunting would push the
deer to these other roads where there were no vehicles. Lastly, getting
a deer out was very easy as well: throw him in the deer cart, and roll
him out. Opening morning found me walking down one of these
roads. As I said, I don't remember how old I was; I know that it is
likely we didn't leave for camp until after my football game, so I had
probably been up pretty late.

When we woke up in the morning, there was always a lot of
discussion about where each of us would go, which road we would
walk down, and how we planned to hunt. My dad gave me my plan,
which at the time I was never too keen on, but I followed it. It wasn't

like I knew any better. So here I was hunting down this road amid the ponderosa pines. My grandpa was a road over, probably not walking too much, but I knew having him on the road over was probably not a bad thing. You see, my grandpa couldn't feel his feet very well, so when he walked, he stomped to feel the ground. Hunting was rough for him, but he usually would move the deer pretty well. I had been walking for about an hour when I saw movement off to my left; a little forked horn buck was bounding through the trees in my direction.

I put my rifle up, waiting for him to slow down, but he didn't. He was cruising and was going to keep on going. I followed him, slow breaths, and squeezed the trigger. The shot fired, and I watched as he dropped almost immediately. I was ecstatic. He was the first deer that I had shot all by myself and it was also a running shot and I knew many in my family heard the shot. I walked over to my deer and sat down. The initial period after the shot can be hard to do things. I was shaking from the adrenaline and was a little in shock, so I just needed to sit there for a moment. I don't know how long I sat there, but it wasn't too long before I could hear those familiar stomps. Grandpa was on his way.

My grandpa and I had a special relationship. I told you earlier that my parents were divorced when I was very young, and my dad was a hard worker. When I was eleven, I went to live with my dad— he moved in with my grandparents—so I spent a lot of hours with my Grandpa Mel. During the summer, we would spend almost the whole day together. He would take me to the doughnut shop where we would sit with all of his old buddies, drink coffee, and shoot the bull. After that, we would go back home, do yard work, watch old John Wayne movies, and hang out. He was, in many ways, my best friend at that time. So when I heard the thuds of his feet coming down the road, I couldn't help but straighten my back, pull my gun belt off, and get ready to tell the story. I could see him; he had my Uncle Stan with him. They had both heard the shot and came to see if I needed help.

Stan yelled, "Did you get him?"

I yelled back almost immediately with a resounding, "You bet."

I was still pretty adrenaline-filled, so I hadn't even started dressing out the deer when they got there. I knew how, but I had never done it on my own. Uncle Stan began to do that work; although he would make me do it, he was letting me have my moment.

Grandpa sat down next to me on the log and said, "Nice deer. How did you get him?"

I retold the story, not leaving any of the fun out especially because he was running and I got him with one shot. It was one of the proudest moments of my life because I got to share it with my grandfather.

We dressed out the deer; Uncle Stan helped me so I didn't mess it up too bad and then left to finish his morning hunt since it was still early. Grandpa and I walked back to camp to get the cart. It was a proud moment for both of us. When we got back to camp, I grabbed the cart. Grandpa asked if I needed his help, and I said I could get it by myself, so he stayed back at camp while I took the cart to get the deer.

I loaded up the deer and walked back to camp; it wasn't that far, but by the time I got back to camp, breakfast was ready, and everyone else was back. I felt like the guy who just hit the walk-off homer in the seventh game of the world series. My dad was there by now and was beaming. He came right over, patted me on the back and said, "Nice buck, son." It was one of those moments. I was so excited, but I could tell almost immediately that my dad was the proudest person in camp. We walked over to the meat pole, and Dad said, "Let's eat, then we will get your deer finished up." I spent all of the breakfast sharing the story, and my dad listened to every word.

This moment, I think, sticks because it is a moment in my life where I reached a new milestone. I had achieved harvesting my first deer on my own; I had hunted it, shot it, and brought it back to camp. These moments come and go, but they are essential to the person achieving them and those who have done the work to get them to that point.

There is a person in the Bible that personifies this as well, and his name was Timothy. Timothy was one of Paul's disciples who had possibly decided to follow Jesus on Paul's first missionary journey. He was probably in his teens or early twenties when he joined Paul on his mission work. Timothy is known for being Paul's representative in several churches and was the pastor at the church in Ephesus. Paul refers to Timothy as a son in 1 Timothy 1:2; he also spends a lot of time mentoring Timothy through his letters, but it is clear that they spent a lot of time together on trips. Paul mentions Timothy being with him in several of his New Testament letters—2 Corinthians, Philippians, Colossians, 1 and 2 Thessalonians, and Philemon—so it is clear that Paul and Timothy spent time together and that Timothy was a blessing to Paul.

But Timothy had parents. Paul mentions them in 2 Timothy 1:3–5:

> I thank God, whom I serve, as my ancestors did, with a clear conscience, as night and day I constantly remember you in my prayers. Recalling your tears, I long to see you, so that I may be filled with joy. I am reminded of your sincere faith, which first lived in your grandmother Lois and in your mother Eunice and, I am persuaded, now lives in you also.

Here we are given a glimpse into who might be more proud than Paul of Timothy: His mother and his grandmother, who raised Timothy in the faith, a sincere faith. It doesn't say anything about his father; obviously, he had one, but whether or not he was around is a guess. What we do know is that Lois and Eunice raised Timothy with a sincere faith. How proud do you think they were of this young man? Yet they likely had no idea just what an essential part of church history Timothy would be. I am sure that they were proud of the young man who had grown to teach others about the love of Jesus.

This brings us to Psalm 127:3:

> Children are a heritage from the Lord, offspring a reward from him.

Let me start by talking about the word *heritage*. The word *heritage* is translated here from the idea of an inheritance. I had always considered an inheritance as something that I would receive when someone passed away. I inherited three things from my grandpa when he passed away: a flannel shirt, a chord jacket, and a red crusher hat. These things hold value to me not because they are worth a lot of money or because they are fantastic art pieces; they have value to me because of who they belonged to. I care for them, and sometimes I look at them and remember my grandfather. I can remember each of these items being worn by him at one time or another, and those memories bring me joy. It is interesting to think of children as an inheritance, and I don't believe that we do that often enough.

If children are a heritage or inheritance from the Lord, that means they belonged to him first. We don't do anything to get them. I know that sounds weird. We do *something* to get them, but the work of making and forming them is God's. We may provide the genes, we may provide the nutrients for them to grow, but they are God's first and foremost. If God made them, and they were his to start with, where does their value reside? Far too often, I hear parents complain about their children or lift them more than they need to be. Let me explain.

I told you about my inheritance from my grandpa. I would probably not go out and buy any of those items at a store, but they hold more value than anything at any store I could go to. Why? Because they belonged to Grandpa. The same is true of children. No matter their talent level, their brains, or their looks, they are valuable.

One of the issues I have in our culture today is that we have placed the wrong value on children. Just like we have decided that it is our job to provide and our job to protect, we value children based on who they are, not whose they are. Our children have a value that goes beyond earthly worth because they are God's workmanship. Ephesians 2:10 states, "For we are his workmanship, created in Christ Jesus for good works, which God prepared beforehand, that we should walk in them." Since we have inherited them, it is our job to admire them and remember their worth in Christ. What does that look like?

It means we don't look to our children to increase our pride in ourselves. Our children are not a means to prove that we are worthy. I am sure I will step on some toes here, mine included. We live in a world that rewards hard work, high achievement, and rare talent. So guess what? Our children receive rewards for hard work, high achievement, and rare talent not just by the world but by us as their parents. We show up at sports events and watch as our son or daughter either succeed or struggle. I see parents arguing with teenage referees and umpires over calls. Angry phone calls from parents litter coach voicemails as parents demand more playing time. The news recently reported, and we watched as we learned parents figured out a way to cheat so their children could go to the best colleges.

Meanwhile, children are experiencing more anxiety and depression than at any other time in history. The drive to be the highest achiever or the best at a sport has caused them to lose their childhood. It bothers me more when I know that the children of our evangelical churches often struggle the most. It makes me sad that the evangelical community has become a breeding ground for success theology, which I won't get into now. Still, evangelical Christians are the worst at having unreasonable career expectations, perfect marriages, and super parenting skills. Yet children are a heritage from the Lord. They are not to be our pride and joy based on their accomplishments. We can be excited and proud when they achieve, but it shouldn't be the end goal.

God gives us these inheritances to pass on a legacy. That legacy is to be a light in the darkness, a hope for a broken world, and a reflection of God and how amazing he is. These inheritances are not just for individual parents. They are for the church—God's church. There must be a premium put on the children so that the church is effective in the future. I have heard so many pray for revival, but then they ignore our children and teens; this must be addressed moving forward. Our children are a heritage from the Lord, and they must be encouraged to point the lost to the glory of the one who created them. That heritage must not be wasted so that we can feel good about ourselves. Instead, they must be taught to be a reflection of their heavenly Father. It is the role of the parents, the church, and the entire community to make this a reality. When my children see the flannel or the jacket, I tell them about the man who owned them before me. Our children need to be taught whose they are so they can tell the lost about God.

Chapter 8

Reaping the Rewards

Offspring, a reward from Him.
—Psalm 127:3b

I don't fish much anymore. I do go fishing, but I don't fish much. I spend most of my time getting all the kids fishing instead of fishing myself. One of my favorite memories occurred during one of those fishing times.

There is a lake not too far from where we live that has some good trout fishing; it can be a little crowded, but it is close to home and holds a fair amount of fish, and with a short walk, you can get to a spot that you might get to catch some. One day, I decided to take the whole crew up to that lake to do some fishing. We drove up the one-and-a-half hours to the parking lot, got everybody out of the vehicles, grabbed poles, tackle boxes, coolers, hats, sunscreen, and even sunglasses, and headed out to our little sweet spot. The walk there was an adventure in itself; Cora would get distracted, Phoebe would yell at Cora, various others in the group would interact as we took a walk around the lake to the backside. We finally got to our particular little spot.

Now, it is crucial to let you know about this little spot. When the water is high, you can see straight down into the water an almost vertical drop-off, which is scary when you have a four-year-old, but it really is a neat spot to fish, so I keep my eyes on Cora very carefully.

Once we arrived, my work began. First, I had to get all the kids fishing, and of course, I hadn't prepared, so it was quite an ordeal. Start with Cora, the four-year-old, who has a princess pole; tie everything together, and get her oldest sister to take her to a spot to fish. Next, Phoebe, the eight-year-old, knows how to do a little more than the four-year-old. I get her all rigged up, and she can cast her own, but I have to keep a watchful eye. Then it is time for Nehemiah, the eleven-year-old. He is far more knowledgeable than the other two but still requires some help.

Just about the time I am ready to relax, *boom*, Cora catches a fish. Good and bad here—Cora catches the first fish, so she is delighted, but in her opinion, we are done fishing. Oh, and she wants to be called the fishing queen, and she gets to pick where we eat lunch. So I finally get her fish off the line, and Phoebe has one on; meanwhile, Elsie, the fifteen-year-old, has dropped her phone into the water in dramatic fashion while trying to film her catching her fish because the world must know. Oh, wait, Nehemiah is now catching a fish. Phoebe needs help getting her pole back out, and Elsie, Maryruth, Derek, and Harmony are laughing at the Elsie debacle and enjoying a thunderous moment. You can imagine that it didn't take long for anyone thinking about coming to that end of the lake to think twice about it. Yes, we are that family.

The day continued like that—just a lot of laughter, a lot of fish and all; even the fishing queen had a great time. We finished up, went into town, got some pizza at a local establishment, and went down by the river to eat it. It was, without a doubt, a great day. Not that it didn't have some frustration; as I said, I didn't get to fish, but being there with all my kids, including my future son-in-law, was remarkable. I couldn't help but feel blessed and rewarded. The reward was definitely the smiles on their faces, the joy in their eyes, and the love in their hearts. I could fully understand how this verse fits right here for this time.

Sometimes rewards are not as easy to come by. Let me take you back to the Old Testament to a girl named Esther. Esther's story is one of great struggle and great reward. Let me share. A king named Xerxes was quite proud of himself so much so he held a festival, and it says he drank for seven days. On the seventh day, he called for his queen, Queen Vashti, to come and be with him. She refused. This moment might be one of my favorite and interesting moments in this story. The king sought out wise counsel concerning what he needed to do to Queen Vashti. The wise counsel was pretty clear that what Queen Vashti had done was not okay. Her disobedience needed to be handled, or all the women in the land would start disobeying their husbands, which would be very bad. So after wise counsel, King Xerxes cast out Queen Vashti.

I want to interrupt the story to point out that I don't think all accounts in the Bible display the best character traits. Women are often mistreated in the Bible and throughout the history of the world. In this story, we must understand how women were treated and their expectations to understand Esther's role and that we can also understand how brave she was. Back to the story.

After several days, the king decided he needed another queen. It is at this point in the story that we meet Mordecai and Esther. Mordecai was a Jewish man who had been brought to Susa while he was in exile. He had a niece that he had taken in as his daughter, treated like a daughter. Her name was Esther. Esther was beautiful, and when the king ordered that all virgins be brought to the palace to stand before the king, Mordecai took her. She was entrusted to a man named Hegai, who got her beauty treatments, gave her the best food, and provided seven attendants to help her through this process. Then Hegai placed Esther and her attendants in the best place in the harem.

Mordecai had told Esther not to reveal her nationality. He forbade her to reveal that she was of Jewish descent. Mordecai was very concerned with her, and it says he paced back and forth in the courtyard every day to find out how she was doing. For twelve months, Esther was pampered and given anything she wanted. She was eventually placed in front of King Xerxes, and he was attracted to Esther more than any other virgin he had been presented. He put a crown on her head and made her queen. Esther remained obedient to Mordecai and never revealed her family background or nationality.

Mordecai becomes a rather prominent piece of the story here as he reveals a plot to assassinate the king. Esther was able to alert the king and gave credit to Mordecai. Now here is where things get complicated. A man named Haman had been given a very high place in the king's court. When Haman heard that Mordecai would not kneel in the king's honor and was disobeying the king because he was a Jew, Haman became enraged; but rather than just deal with Mordecai, Haman decided the best thing to do was kill all the Jewish people. He went to the king:

> Then Haman said to King Xerxes, "There is a certain people dispersed among the peoples in all the provinces of your kingdom who keep themselves separate. Their customs are different from those of all other people, and they do not obey the king's laws; it is not in the king's best interest to tolerate them. If it pleases the king, let a decree be issued to destroy them, and I will give ten thousand talents of silver to the king's administrators for the royal treasury." (Esther 3:8–9)

So Haman's goal was to destroy all of the Jewish people. The king accepted his request and then sent out a proclamation that would carry out Haman's wishes as his own.

This proclamation caused great distress among the Jews. Mordecai was so upset he tore his clothes, put on sackcloth, and the Bible says he walked around waling and weeping. One of Esther's attendants told Esther about Mordecai, which caused Esther to be in distress. She sent clothes for Mordecai to wear, but he refused them. Esther sent another attendant to find out what was wrong. Mordecai explained to the attendant what had happened and then asked if the attendant would relay the message to Esther to go to the king and beg for mercy. Esther responded by telling Mordecai that the king would kill her if she went in front of him without being summoned. Mordecai then responds that her silence would not save her if this proclamation continued.

It is at this point that Esther decides to give it a shot. She told Mordecai to gather all the Jews and fast for three days. After three days, Esther put on her royal robes and entered the inner court of the king's hall. When the king saw her, he was pleased with her and invited her in. Then he said, "What is it, Queen Esther? What is your request? Even up to half the kingdom, it will be given you."

Queen Esther invited the king and Haman to a banquet. The king and Haman went to the feast, where the king asked Esther again what she wanted. Esther asked that they would come to a second banquet the next day. Esther 5:9–14 says,

> Haman went out that day happy and in high spirits. But when he saw Mordecai at the king's gate and observed that he neither rose nor showed fear in his presence, he was filled with rage against Mordecai. Nevertheless, Haman restrained himself and went home.
>
> Calling together his friends and Zeresh, his wife, Haman boasted to them about his vast wealth, his many sons, and all the ways the king had honored him and how he had elevated him above the other nobles and officials. "And that's not all," Haman added. "I'm the only person Queen Esther invited to accompany the king to the banquet she gave. And she has invited me along with the king tomorrow. But all this gives me no satisfaction as long as I see that Jew Mordecai sitting at the king's gate."
>
> His wife Zeresh and all his friends said to him, "Have a pole set up, reaching to a height of fifty cubits, and ask the king in the morning to have Mordecai impaled on it. Then go with the king to the banquet and enjoy yourself." This suggestion delighted Haman, and he had the pole set up.

God had different plans. That night, the king asked for a history of his kingship read to him, and when the part about Mordecai saving his life came up, the king realized he had not honored Mordecai for what he had done. The next day, Xerxes asked Haman what he would do to honor someone that had pleased him. Haman, thinking Xerxes was talking about him, answered with an elaborate celebration described in Esther 6:7–9:

> For the man the king delights to honor, have them bring a royal robe the king has worn and a horse the king has ridden, one with a royal crest placed on its head. Then let the robe and horse be entrusted to one of the king's most noble princes. Let them robe the man the king delights to honor, and lead him on the horse through the city streets, proclaiming before him, "This is what is done for the man the king delights to honor!"

Xerxes told Haman that he would like that done to Mordecai, so Haman had to dress Mordecai in robes and ride him down the streets on a horse to honor him. So instead of impaling Mordecai, Haman was honoring Mordecai. Soon after that, Haman was at the dinner table with Xerxes and Esther. When it came time for Esther to reveal what she was requesting. She asked the king to spare her people from death and annihilation. When he asked who did this, she told him it was Haman. The king was enraged, and Haman was killed with the pole he had picked to impale Mordecai on.

Esther and Mordecai continued to speak to the king and continued to get things done for the Jews. In the end, Esther and Mordecai had great rewards. The important thing is to realize that these rewards came directly from God so that he would be glorified.

So what do these stories have to do with the phrase "offspring, a reward from him"? They show how the way that we raise our children can bring us great rewards. My story shows that our children will bring us joy. The story of Esther shows that raising a child well can have great rewards, but that may not be the point of this sentence.

In the last chapter, I talked about children being a heritage or an inheritance. Here we see that they are a reward. The inheritance aspect talks about where they come from—God; the reward talks about how they come. Let me explain. Some inheritances are bad. I inherited a receding hairline, and I inherited a short stature. I have seen many movies over the years where people inherit a house that is in ruins. The point is that there are some things you inherit that are not good. Children are not one of those things. Children are a heritage and a reward.

Who doesn't like a reward? A reward, in its very definition, is something that people would like. It is defined as a gift given in recognition of an effort, achievement, or service. I received an award recently, celebrating my tenth year of service at the church where I serve. It was a great reward. I was thankful for it and was excited to go and enjoy it. We often see rewards posted for finding animals. There are stories about someone giving an excellent bonus for a person doing the right thing. There are so many ways for us to look at rewards, but in the end, they are good. So, if children are an excellent inheritance, what does that mean for us when it comes time to raising or growing them?

Here we go, or at least here is what this says to me. Bear with me a little on this because where I go with this might seem a little fantastic. God is our heavenly Father. He has a gift for each one of us—not just any gift. God doesn't give us the keys to shed out back and say, "Hey, whatever you find out there, you can have." Instead, God has his most unique gift, a gift that he formed, a gift that he loves. It is something so precious that he doesn't want to give it to anyone else. He has picked you, and it is good, very good. As he hands this gift off to you, he whispers in their ear what Jeremiah 1:5 says, "Before I formed you in the womb I knew you, before you were born I set you apart." Then he gives the child to us—a good gift that we get to enjoy.

When you accept the inheritance, the excellent gift, or reward, you take the responsibility of caring for it with the idea that it will carry on the legacy of God. I want to be clear here: I don't mean our heritage or the important traditions to your family or community or culture. The most important thing we can do is make sure that we are moving the children we care for in the direction of God, carrying on the message that God wants the whole world to hear, making sure they understand where they come from and to whom they belong.

We must realize that for the Israelites, children were the quintessential reward. The goal of a child born in the Israelite nation was to grow and carry on God's Word. Of course, the Israelites didn't always do a great job at this. We can see throughout the Old Testament where the Israelite nation failed to teach their children. Yet the instructions were clear in Deuteronomy 6: 4–9:

> Hear, O Israel: The Lord our God, the Lord is one. Love the Lord your God with all your heart and with all your soul and with all your strength. These commandments that I give you today are to be on your hearts. Impress them on your children. Talk about them when you sit at home and when you walk along the road, when you lie down and when you get up. Tie them as symbols on your hands and bind them on your foreheads. Write them on the doorframes of your houses and on your gates.

This passage gives clear instructions on how we are to care for our children because they are God's. If this is the case, why doesn't it happen?

I think at least a part of that is that we don't see our children as rewards. The world has taken the joy of having children away. In first-world developed countries like America, it is especially true. For the most part, Evangelical America has decided that wealth and wealth management are the keys to a healthy home. I don't want to be mean here, but I have to speak what I see and hear. The average family in America has less than two children, the average age of retirement is sixty-one, and the average sales price of a new home is close to 400k. So, if you are an average person in America, you will stop having children at forty; you probably won't start until you are close to thirty. You will have one, maybe two children, and you build a lot of monetary wealth. What is wrong with that? Well, on the surface, nothing. (Please continue reading. I'm not trying to beat up on the American way or financial health. I am just making it a point that we no longer view children as a reward.) Everyone looks happy. Commercials show us in our boats and RVs living the high life.

Meanwhile, we hear things like the family is breaking down, Jesus is no longer the center of our American way of life. At least part of that is we no longer view children as an inheritance or a reward but instead as a burden. Our lifestyles have made it more important to *provide* (again, not our job) our children with the best—the best house, the best car, the best school, and the best friends. Because the world is a terrible place, you better make sure you can *protect* (also not our job) so that the children we have are comfortable and happy, and then after we are done caring for them and making sure they are well taken care of, we can be satisfied because we will be able to build our wealth and retire like kings.

One of the most significant weaknesses in the church of tomorrow will be the lack of people to fill them. The Bible does not beat around the bush when it talks about children. They are a heritage and a reward from God. I also believe that the Bible is clear that we should have a lot of children. I have lived out this in my life. I will tell you why. I will also talk about it more in the following chapters, but I want to use the Bible to give you some insight.

Genesis 1:28 states,

> And God said to them, "Be fruitful and multiply and fill the earth and subdue it and have dominion over the fish of the sea and over the birds of the heavens and over every living thing that moves on the earth."

Psalm 128:3 states,

> Your wife will be like a fruitful vine within
> your house; your children will be like olive shoots
> around your table.

Proverbs 17:6:

> Grandchildren are the crown of the aged,
> and the glory of children is their fathers.

If we had a healthy view of children in our lives as rewards, wouldn't we want many of them? I think the only answer is yes.

So I know what you are thinking; at least I will claim to know what you are thinking. Yes, raising children is hard. It can be expensive, it can be tiring, and it can wear you out. I believe that those are all the reasons able people don't have children.

I want to stop here and talk to couples who can't conceive. This verse might be a hard one for you. I will never claim to understand your pain; however, I believe that you can adopt and that you are so blessed if you choose to do that. There are many in my church that are foster parents and have adopted many children. Those children are being raised and loved by parents who have it to give. Let me also encourage you to work with children, volunteer at your church, volunteer in the community. I will talk about the idea of how it takes a village later, but you can be an essential part of taking the rewards God gives us and helping to groom them into the people God uses.

I speak from experience when I tell you that all of those reasons are valid. Children are a lot of work—work that never ends. They are expensive, and they are a pain in the rear sometimes, but they are a reward. We have six children—seven if you count my son-in-law— and I have one grandchild, Bowen, my grandson, Bowen is the reason that I will count Derek among our children. Just kidding. Derek is a great son-in-law, and I would count him without the grandchild. There have been times in my life I think about all that we might have if we didn't have so many children. Maybe I would hunt more, and perhaps I would take trips to Africa or Europe. Perhaps I would have a newer truck or a nicer house? Maybe I would have more spending power? All of those questions have one problem: they include the word *I*. Another book I read once started with the phrase "It's not about you." This statement couldn't be more accurate. This world and our reason for existing in it is about glorifying God, and if children are a reward from him, then we should treat them as such. Be aware that your children are not just your rewards. All children are a reward to all people, and how we treat that reward will be the factor in how that reward treats us.

Chapter 9

Did I Hit Where I Was Aiming?

Like arrows in the hands of a warrior.
—Psalm 127:4a

The first time I went shopping for a bow, I had no idea what I was doing. I had always hunted with a rifle and had decided to give archery hunting a shot through some interesting circumstances (no pun intended). I went through the phone book. At this time, the Internet was still in its early stages, so the phone book was the best option. I found several bow shops in the Phoenix area, chose the one closest, and drove there one day after work. When I walked in, I was greeted with a vast array of bows, archery equipment, and hunting gear. It was rather daunting at first glance. Guys were walking to and from the back with their bows in hand, sharing greetings and salutations with the man at the counter, so it took him a moment to greet me.

I let him know what I was doing, how I was a beginner, and that I wanted to shoot an animal in three months. He didn't laugh. Honestly, I would today if someone said that to me. He did not. He said, "All right," and began measuring me. He measured my arms, had me draw back on a bow, which was my first lesson in shooting a bow. Once he had me drawing like I was supposed to, he measured some other things. After doing all of that, he walked me back over to the counter and began showing me his suggested bows. I picked a bow package that included all of the necessary items needed to hunt with that bow.

After we picked the bow, he showed me the arrows that came with the bow. I was excited and ready to start shooting my new bow setup. The salesperson quickly stopped me, letting me know that neither the bow nor the arrows were ready. The shop would have to change out some things on the bow to make the draw length appropriate, and they would have to cut the arrows to match the draw length. I would have to come back in a couple of days to make sure everything worked, and then I could start shooting.

I only hunted with my bow one year. I had fun but felt I was still more of a rifle hunter until I moved to New Mexico. Maybe you are wondering how that happened. Well, let me share. As soon as we moved to New Mexico, I figured out where and when I wanted to hunt. The good news was deer hunting was an over-the-counter tag, and I had heard of an area where there were mountains not too far away that had deer. So, I went and bought my tag and headed out to the woods to do some scouting in the middle of September. I found an old two-track and decided to see what was down at the end of that road. I was quiet, just enjoying the moment, when the mountain came alive. One elk bugled then another and then another. They continued bugling for at least thirty minutes, and I just stood there and listened. Occasionally, I saw something flashing in the trees, but I hadn't seen one of the bulls yet. Then out of nowhere, one stood right in front of me and let out a scream. I was in awe. The amount of adrenaline that dumped through my body caused me to start shaking. I had heard bulls bugle, I had seen bull elk in the wild, but I had never experienced something like this.

Later that year, I asked everyone about elk hunting, I had a lot of questions, and I was given many answers. I came away with the solution: "If you want to hunt when the elk are doing that, you need to bow hunt." Immediately I took my bow out of its case and started shooting. I would shoot every day, and my oldest daughter, Harmony, would come out with me; it wasn't long before she was shooting with me. Jim came out with some excellent little yardage blocks, and we set up a pretty good little shooting range on the property. So we would shoot, I would draw a tag, and I would shoot. During one of these shoots, Harmony asked the question, "Did I shoot where I was aiming?" It was a lot of laughter, but it holds to how we raise kids, and I want to talk about that.

When I went bow shopping, it wasn't just a process of buying the first bow I saw and making that work. The bow, the arrows, really the whole setup was designed with me in mind; it was set to my measurements, and therefore, I would be able to shoot that bow better than someone who wasn't me. It took a lot of work. It didn't just happen. This makes me love this verse so much because you see, arrows aren't just given to us. To understand what I mean, we will have to look at how warriors received arrows.

An archer in biblical times would have had quite a task when it came to getting arrows. The warrior wasn't able to go down to the store, look at the vast amount of graphite arrows on display, see the weight, the length, and the material, and decide which arrows he would buy. No, the warrior was purposeful about his arrows. First, he would find a branch; that branch had to come from a particular tree that made good arrows. He would take that branch, maybe several, and start the process of making his arrows.

Making an arrow was far more than just cutting a branch off a tree, slapping some stuff on it, and seeing how it worked; the warrior was cautious about taking the raw material he had and turning it into a highly tuned instrument. The warrior would get that branch, start by stripping the branch completely, would work tirelessly to make sure that all of the lumps were gone and that he had a smooth arrow shaft. The warrior didn't want anything on it to be affected by the small currents, so it needed to be smooth. It could take hours getting the arrow to be smooth and free of extra hindrances.

Then the warrior would work on making the arrow straight. The warrior would have to heat and cool the arrow many times, each time working on making the arrow as straight as possible. The warrior didn't want the arrow to wobble during the shot, making it more apt to miss the target; making the arrow shaft in itself would have taken a lot of time. When the warrior had finished the shaft, he would have to gather the proper fletching, cut it, shape it, and put it on the arrow. After the warrior had cut, shaped, and added the fletching, it was time to pick the arrowhead. The warrior was again careful about his choices. He was careful about what the arrow would be used for; after choosing an arrowhead and shaping the arrowhead, he would place the arrowhead on the arrow, making it ready for use.

The warrior didn't do this just once; the warrior would do this over and over again, and each time, the warrior would use the same process and would create the same arrow over and over again. Those arrows may not be perfectly the same, but the warrior would make sure that they would shoot the same and head in the right direction. The warrior would never ask the question, "Did I hit where I was aiming?" Instead, he nurtured and built the arrows with a particular target in mind. So it is with raising children. All of us should be keenly aware that the Bible is not trying to be cool here by using arrows as an analogy; it is meant to help us understand the importance of raising God's heritage and his reward.

One of my favorite stories about raising children is found in the story of Samuel in 1 Samuel. The story goes like this: There was a woman named Hannah, who was married to a man named Elkanah. Elkanah had two wives (I don't make this stuff up, I promise), Peninnah and Hannah. Peninnah had children, and Hannah did not. Now, Elkanah loved Hannah and was sad for her that God had "closed her womb," but Peninnah was mean to her.

First Samuel 1:6 states,

> Because the Lord had closed Hannah's womb, her rival kept provoking her in order to irritate her.

Hannah was sorrowful; for the sake of realizing just how clueless men are, I would like to take a moment to discuss the men mentioned here in this story. Elkanah asks Hannah why she is so upset, saying, "Hannah, why are you weeping? Why don't you eat? Why are you downhearted? Don't I mean more to you than ten sons?" Eli, the priest, who would eventually help in the raising of Samuel, told her one day while she was praying, "How long are you going to stay drunk? Put away your wine." Neither of these men understood just how upset Hannah was.

Hannah didn't give up though. She prayed and she prayed. She went as far as to make a vow. She said,

> Lord Almighty, if you will only look on your servant's misery and remember me, and not forget your servant, but give her a son, then I will give him to the Lord for all the days of his life.

Hannah's prayer was answered, and she was given a son that she named Samuel. She named him Samuel because she asked the Lord for him.

This is where Samuel's story takes shape. Hannah had promised to dedicate Samuel to God, so shortly after Samuel was weaned, he was taken to the house of the Lord. It was here that Samuel grew up—some interesting tidbits here. Eli's sons were not good, and because of that, Eli knew his time was short, and God told Eli that his family would not continue in the priesthood. However, Eli raised Samuel and taught him all that he needed to know. You might know the story of when the Lord called Samuel; the account is found in 1 Samuel 3:2–13:

> One night Eli, whose eyes were becoming so weak that he could barely see, was lying down in his usual place. The lamp of God had not yet gone out, and Samuel was lying down in the house of the Lord, where the ark of God was. Then the Lord called Samuel.
>
> Samuel answered, "Here I am." And he ran to Eli and said, "Here I am; you called me."
>
> But Eli said, "I did not call; go back and lie down." So he went and lay down. Again the Lord called, "Samuel!" And Samuel got up and went to Eli and said, "Here I am; you called me."

"My son," Eli said, "I did not call; go back and lie down."

Now Samuel did not yet know the Lord: The word of the Lord had not yet been revealed to him.

A third time the Lord called, "Samuel!" And Samuel got up and went to Eli and said, "Here I am; you called me."

Then Eli realized that the Lord was calling the boy. So Eli told Samuel, "Go and lie down, and if he calls you, say, 'Speak, Lord, for your servant is listening.'" So Samuel went and lay down in his place.

The Lord came and stood there, calling as at the other times, "Samuel! Samuel!"

Then Samuel said, "Speak, for your servant is listening."

And the Lord said to Samuel: "See, I am about to do something in Israel that will make the ears of everyone who hears about it tingle. At that time I will carry out against Eli everything I spoke against his family—from beginning to end. For I told him that I would judge his family forever because of the sin he knew about; his sons blasphemed God, and he failed to restrain them. Therefore I swore to the house of Eli, 'The guilt of Eli's house will never be atoned for by sacrifice or offering.'"

In the morning, Eli asked Samuel what the Lord had said. Samuel did not want to, but after some convincing, he told Eli what God had said. Eli's reaction was pretty good. He said that God was the Lord, let Him do what is good in his eyes.

Samuel becomes a great prophet, and in fact, he is heavily involved in naming Israel's first king, Saul, and calling David king.

I think this story helps to illustrate the idea of children as arrows because you see a mom who follows through on her commitment, and we see a man, who frankly didn't do well with his sons, shape and develop one of the great prophets of Israel. This story is proof that purposeful arrows bring blessings.

What culture taught me about raising children

I was raised in an environment that was different than many of my friends. I told you before that my parents were divorced when I was five years old, so that made my experience different than some of my friends. Many of my friends' moms stayed home while the dad worked, which didn't look like my family. Many of the moms were home when my friends got home, which didn't look like my family. It didn't upset me, and it still doesn't, but it was just my life. I didn't know any different. I had seen different on TV and saw different in my friends' lives, but it didn't bother me.

By the time Tamra and I were married, I had seen some new things. I started to believe some things about parenting that were taught to me. This sort of goes back to the first part of the passage, so just let me lead you to my natural conclusion. As a husband, it was my job to provide, it was my job to protect, and it was my job to *stress*. Through all of my different mentors and preaching, I learned that I was the man; therefore, I did man things. This meant that it was the wife's job to care for our children. It was Tamra's job to nurture them. I was to bring discipline, and she was to bring love. I saw this played out all around me in various ways, but it says something very different when you look at this verse. It says that the children are like arrows in the hands of a warrior.

Warrior

In this portion of the verse, we meet a warrior. The warrior is not given a gender. I think this is very important. It is essential because to me, it is evident that warriors are not gender specific. There were plenty of women in the Bible who would have been considered warriors. I don't want to get on some soapbox about gender equality here because that is not the point. The point is that there is no gender associated with the warrior. Along with that, though, I believe that this is written with the idea that males would need to hear this more than women; the word *warrior* attracts more males to what is being said, and I think it makes a point to that.

The original readers would have understood the process of arrow making. The heritage and reward that we have been given was going to require nurturing. That nurturing wasn't going to come from the dad; it was going to come from the warrior. I do believe that men are the culprits of being poor nurturers though. Let me explain. When it comes to raising children, men often are tasked with the manly things especially in the church. I have been in many conversations about the absent fathers, so kids are not getting what only fathers can give. Of course, I struggle with this idea, but I also think it is important to note. The father is an essential part of raising the children but not because he is rougher or can teach the children how to do certain things. It is because God shows us that warriors are a part of the nurturing process. I think the cultural norm says Dad's discipline and mom's nurture are not biblical and should be stated.

This verse tells me that a cultural norm is not always the best. I have seen, time and time again, sons and daughters whose relationships with their fathers are distant and painful not because their fathers are mean but because the father was not involved in the soft shaping of the child's heart and soul. I look at the warrior with his arrows, and I see someone deeply involved in the process of shaping a child. If children are arrows, then it is our job—mom, dad, uncle, grandparents, and community, which includes church—to carefully cut off the parts that will be moved by the currents, heat, and cool so that they are straight and, finally, clothe them with the proper fletching and arrowhead. It is the warrior's job, and the warrior is the one who has access to the arrow (child).

How do we do this?

I will do some soapbox standing here and will not apologize for it. The question of how is quite simple yet at the same time quite consuming. Deuteronomy 6:4–7 states,

> Hear, O Israel: The Lord our God, the Lord is one. Love the Lord your God with all your heart and with all your soul and with all your strength. These commandments that I give you today are to be on your hearts. Impress them on your children. Talk about them when you sit at home and when you walk along the road, when you lie down and when you get up.

This is the first and most important process of arrow making—to love the Lord, to love his Word, and to impress them on your children. I can't stress this enough. I know single moms who have raised amazing young men and women. I know single dads who have raised amazing young men and women.

I believe there are three vitally important aspects to nurturing children that will help them become smooth straight arrows.

1. Make sure you (the warrior) are reading your Bible. Find a way to spend at least five minutes with his Word. There are many apps out there that can make this pretty easy, but it is vitally important to do it.
2. Get you and your children to church. I know that the church has taken a hit over the past several years, but it is still the best place for your family, whatever it looks like, to be. Ensure your children are involved in peer groups at the church, children's ministry, student ministry, and young adult ministry. Make going to church a habit, and do it even if you don't want to.
3. Make sure you have other warriors that you can depend on to help you shape and straighten your children. If you have

at least seven other positive influences on your children, you will see those influences help.

If you are single, don't think you need someone from the opposite sex to help you with things. You are a warrior, God has given you these gifts, and he has given you the ability to meet all their needs as a parent. God knows your situation, and he knows your needs; it is not your job to do everything. Depend on him, and let him do amazing things.

Finally, realize that all of this is dependent on the fact that you are following the earlier verses. Allow God to take care of the provision, the protection, and allow him to bless you in and through your sleep. Then you can take these rewards and shape them into the children God wants them to be—like arrows in the hands of a warrior.

Chapter 10

Oh, to Be Young Again

Are children in one's youth.
—Psalm 127:4b

I got to my spot at the perfect time. It was cool, it was dark, and I would be to the clearing by the spring in enough time to hopefully catch a bull going to or coming from his water in the morning. It was going to be hot pretty soon this morning. The forecast called for a temperature in the low nineties. I had only seen this place I was going to once, but I did love it and felt very comfortable that it would be fruitful.

I gathered all my gear, locked the truck, and checked that all my equipment was inside. Finally, I checked for my release, my arrows. My backpack was secure; I was ready to go. I walked up that hill pretty fast. The two-track I was going to follow was just on the other side. I would use my flashlight sparingly to make sure I didn't break an ankle or something. When I got to the top of the hill, I pulled my phone out to make sure I was going in the right direction; after dropping it and making sure it was still okay, I kept on plugging away. I finally hit the two-track and began following it. It had been a dry year in New Mexico, the monsoon didn't produce much rain, which meant that there was no green grass in most areas; but in this valley, there was green grass.

I walked along very quietly, and I would cow call now and then, see if I could get something to respond. I wanted to be in a particular spot when it got light, so I didn't spend too much time waiting for responses; plus, I didn't want to be sneaking in the heat. I hoped to accomplish the majority of the climb while it was still cool outside.

I got to the top pretty fast, and there with a beautiful meadow hidden from the rest of the area. It was a perfect little setting. The dew was shimmering in the first light, and the air was even a little cooler here. I felt like I had reached a good destination. I just knew there would be elk here. I sat at the edge and waited for enough light to see something moving. I was feeling good, there had been plenty of tracks leading here, and I knew that the spring was close. The wind wasn't quite right, so I snuck to a group of trees out across the meadow. I was slowly moving and watching when I saw movement to my left. My heart started beating, praying it hadn't seen me. It hadn't, but it also wasn't an elk. It was a bear. I let the bear move out of sight and continued to my next spot. I looked to the left and saw a pretty fresh rub; again, I could feel the excitement. It was clear that the elk were using this spot, and I was feeling excited.

I felt that I had snuck in here without disturbing anything and felt very good, so I stood right next to the rub and did a call sequence. (A call sequence is when you make different elk calls to imitate what a herd of elk might sound like.) I started with a couple of soft cow calls followed by a couple that were a little louder and then ended with a slight chuckle. (A chuckle is a sound a bull elk makes for various reasons but doesn't mean anything, kind of like saying, "Good morning.")

Nothing responded, so I sat for a few minutes and listened to the sounds of the forest. The birds were pretty active especially in the trees surrounding this clearing. I began to look around and could see just how excellent this little spot was. I decided to do another sequence; this time, I did a few cow calls, a few calf calls, and ended with a high-pitched bugle. Immediately I got a response, and he was close. The adrenaline started pumping. He was just up where I had seen that bear, so I checked the wind and got to a spot where he wouldn't be able to smell me if he came closer. I moved and bugled again and got an immediate response. I continued this for a few minutes, and it was evident to me he was not coming closer.

In situations like this, the best thing to do is close the gap. I very carefully started up the ridge, slowly creeping and looking. I kept listening for rocks moving or breathing—anything to give me a hint of where he was. Nothing. I just kept moving as slow as I could, then I looked to my left; and there he was, staring right at me. I tried to get a shot off, but he didn't want to stick around. He didn't crash off, so I thought maybe he didn't go too far.

I moved up to the top of the ridge and found an excellent spot to sit and listen. I knew the spring was just off to my left, and this bull may have been going there, so I might be able to get a chance still if I was quiet. After about thirty minutes, I decided to try a bugle to see what would happen. Three bulls bugled back, and I was at full alert again. The bull from earlier had not gone far, and two others were up the mountain on the other side of the spring. I didn't exactly know what to do, but I knew staying here and doing nothing would not work, I decided to see if I could get another response, and I did. The close bull must have decided to leave, but I had two other bulls, and I would go after them.

I started toward the other bulls. It was starting to get warm now. The sun was up, and as I began to move toward the two other bulls, I had a feeling that I hadn't ever felt before—the question: "Do I want to work that hard just to see if I can get close?" Those two bulls were up a pretty steep grade, and it was getting pretty hot. It didn't take long before my decision was made. I was going to call and see if they would come down. I was not interested in taking that hike.

Of course, it didn't work. Eventually, they both stopped calling, and I took my walk downhill, back to the air-conditioned truck. When I was younger, which wasn't that long ago, I wouldn't have even thought twice about going after those two bulls even to see if I could get close. These are the things that happen. I don't know that it is better to be younger, but it is different, which brings us to this section of the passage.

I almost didn't split this verse into two sections because I couldn't see the inherent value of this portion, but the more I thought about it, the more it caused me to think about what the writer was trying to convey and how it was related to our culture today. I wondered if this statement might be yet another shock to the system that we have developed in today's world that might hinder what God truly wants.

It seems that the world, in general, encourages getting married later and having your first child later in life. In 1920 the average age of someone's first marriage was twenty-one to twenty-two years of age. In 2020 that number fell in at thirty-two. The average age of someone having their first baby in 1920 was about the same age as marriage, twenty-one to twenty-two years old. In 2020, the average age for your first child is now twenty-seven, with many waiting until they are thirty before having children. Several factors lead to these numbers, but I think that the main factor is that we no longer encourage getting married or having children too young.

Tamra and I were very young when we were married. I was twenty, and Tamra was eighteen. Tamra had graduated high school in June, and we were married in July. We accepted a lot of criticism for making that decision and were discouraged. We were told things like finish college, wait until you can afford it, you guys will never make it (we have been married twenty-nine years and counting, have six children, and fall more in love every year). We were discouraged in the same way when we told everyone we were going to have our first baby (the truth is we were discouraged with a lot of our children.) I am not saying it was easy. It was challenging. When you are twenty-two years old, you are clueless. We had no idea what we were doing. We made many dumb mistakes (I still do), but man, the memories are terrific. I tell you this because I think I have some insight into how it all works. We had Harmony in our early twenties, and we had Cora in our early forties.

Would I say that we are better parents now? Would I say we were better parents then? I don't think *better* is the proper term. *Different* is a more accurate description of our parenting now and then. It is my insight that allows me to speak specifically to what I think this verse is saying. I don't believe that this verse says that only young parents will enjoy their children; from personal experience, I would disagree. I think, though, that this verse continues to point out something about our lives and children that is very important; we shouldn't allow anything but the Lord to dictate when and how we have children.

I don't want you to think that I am promoting teenage pregnancy or that I am saying we need to go back to a time when we were marrying off our daughters at fourteen so they could bear many children to a man of our choosing (I am pretty sure the whole Gedde household would revolt against me). I state that we have to stop making up reasons not to have children when our children are younger. I remember when Maryruth and Derek told us they were pregnant. My immediate thoughts were, "They are too young." "They do not have the money." "They haven't been married long enough." Although valid in the world, you can see that those thoughts are not correct with God. God sees them very differently. Why was I, the same guy who is writing this book, having those thoughts? I was having those thoughts because I hadn't given this fantastic young couple over to the Lord. I still wanted to dictate, but I needed to be reminded—"unless the Lord."

Let me tell you about a different young couple. This one is in the Bible, and most of us know them because they are vital figures every year at Christmas—Mary and Joseph. Before I go into too much detail, let me talk about the ages of Mary and Joseph. Some early theologians believed that Joseph was ninety years old when he married Mary. I always had a problem with that age, I know things were different in those days, but that is so wrong on so many levels. The chances of being a single mom have to rise exponentially, and the chances of being a mom at all go down, so it never made sense. I can go along with Joseph being thirty, but that is as far as I will go. However, it is now believed that they were both teenagers; more than likely Mary was fourteen and Joseph was eighteen; of course, these are still estimates, but they are pretty safe estimates based on the cultural norms of that time.

Now, back to the story. If it is okay with you, I will skim over the whole Jesus-was-born story. I think that most of us know it. An essential piece of the birth of Jesus is the age of Mary though. I believe that God chose Mary while she was very young because he knew that (1) she would listen and believe that what the angel told her was real, (2) she would need total dependence on God to succeed in this endeavor, and (3) she was innocent and would trust God. So here you had God choosing a very young couple to be the parents of Jesus. Think about that for just a moment. By the world's standards, they would not have money. They would not have life experiences; in the case of Mary and Joseph, they weren't even married, which, of course, has its own set of problems. So Jesus was born to an unmarried teenage couple. That sounds like a recipe for disaster, but—unless the Lord.

Let's fast forward twelve years, and we see an incredible story about how these young parents did in their daunting task. In the book of Luke chapter 2, a remarkable story is told about Jesus that I think is just as an incredible story about his parents. When Jesus was twelve years old, his parents would go to Jerusalem for the festival of Passover. They did this every year, as was the custom. When they left for home, Jesus stayed behind, but they were unaware of it. After a full day of travel, they realized that Jesus was not with the family. Joseph and Mary traveled back to Jerusalem, where Jesus was sitting in the temple courts, sitting among the teachers. It says that all who heard him were amazed at his understanding and his answers.

When Joseph and Mary found him, they were astonished; but they were still his parents, so they said, "Son, why have you treated us like this? Your father and I have been anxiously searching for you."

Jesus answered and said, "Why were you searching for me? Didn't you know I had to be in my Father's house?"

It says that they didn't fully understand him but that he was obedient and followed them back to Nazareth, where Jesus grew in stature and favor with God and man.

I think this story has a lot to say about what made Mary and Joseph great parents even at their young age. The first thing to note is that Mary and Joseph followed the religious customs with their children in tow. It says they went to the feast every year. They believed that teaching their children the important lessons of God was of the utmost importance. The second thing is that they weren't doing it alone. One of the reasons that Jesus was left behind was because they were with all of their family, and clearly, they were all just taking care of each other's needs. It probably wasn't until dinner time that they noticed Jesus was gone when the family sat down to eat together. Finally, they were teaching Jesus the Bible. I know it is Jesus, and yes, I know that Jesus is an exceptional child, but Mary and Joseph had made it a point to teach Jesus about God using the Torah. So this little passage tells me that what we see as a disaster, Jesus can use to save the world.

So let's get back to our passage. Why is it essential that the writer mentions youth here? I don't think that the writer is telling us to all go out and have children as soon as possible, but I think the writer is trying to make a point. There is something about being young, fresh parents that requires a certain dependence on God and others. Let me explain this by using the two examples I have. When Tamra and I first became parents, we lived in a small two-bedroom apartment, driving subpar vehicles, and had very little money. The dependence on our parents was tremendous. Tamra would call her mom about taking care of the baby, and I would call my mom about taking care of my wife. We needed to trust that God would take care of the finances, the doctor bills, the food, and all that went along with that. We were dependent on our church community to help us by providing an hour a week to spend time together away from Harmony and listen to his Word. Now I look at Derek and Maryruth. Tamra receives phone calls about Bowen a lot, as do I. Although Derek and Maryruth are in a different financial position we were in, they still depend on God and family to make it through this time. The joy that I see and hear in Maryruth and Derek's voices about little Bowen is genuinely remarkable.

Youth doesn't have to mean super young. The older I get, the older young people get. Just the other day, Tamra was referencing the fact that I call thirty-five-year-olds young people. The idea of youth is relative. I think the term *youth* here has more to do with a state of mind, and I also feel that this state of mind must come from the first two verses "unless the Lord."

This small verse packs a punch to me. We live in a world where the most important thing is *me*. I think this is demonstrated in the numbers that I pointed out earlier. As a society, we are getting married later and less. We are having fewer children later. Because of that and other factors, we are watching a community become far less dependent on God. The question is, why? Well, it is simple—we have lost our first love and have lost our way. God's first commandment was to be fruitful and multiply. Throughout the years, we have been told that having children too young is irresponsible; it is harder on children with young parents. We have been told that it costs a lot of money, so we shouldn't burden those around us with the responsibility of our children. I think that God's design is a little different. Go back to Mary and Joseph. Here, a young couple followed the Lord, and the village helped raise the children unless the Lord builds the house.

Our society says that we need to finish college, have a great career before we start having children. Why? So that we can have them in the best schools, so that we can live in safe neighborhoods, so that we can have a healthy bank account to pay the bills, and we can make sure we are building a nest egg that will help us in retirement. God's way looks different. God says that *children* are a heritage, *children* are a reward, and that unless the Lord protects the city, all that we do is in vain.

My point is this—and I want to be careful here—as parents and grandparents, I am not saying that we should push our children to go out and get married and have a child very fast. No, I am trying to say that in God's design, it is not a horrible thing for kids to fall in love and get married. It is good for our young married couples to want to have children and ask us to help them raise them. It is biblical. Let me go off track for a moment. When Tamra and I were married, some people said the only reason we were getting married was to have sex. I don't necessarily disagree with at least a part of that assumption. Tamra and I were deeply in love, and we knew, without a shadow of a doubt, that we wanted to spend the rest of our lives together. So there were two options, one, which would have been looked upon as wise, was for us to wait until we were done with college and then get married. It seems smart, but Tamra and I were determined not to have sex before we were married. I feel confident that if we had said,

"Fine, we will wait until after college to get married," the chances of making it to the honeymoon would have been slim. So yes, we loved each other, we wanted to spend our lives together, and we wanted to have a family together. The only thing that was missing from the equation was sleeping together. I guess what I am saying is that God's design throughout the Bible is pretty straightforward: get married if you are in love. When you get married, make a family. You can wait, but there will always be something else that gets in the way because unless the Lord is the driving factor in your life, you will always find a way to circumvent his way.

Chapter 11

I Forgot the Quiver

Blessed is the man whose quiver is full of them.
—Psalm 127:5a

We got back to camp at about noon. My hunting partner would have to head home, and I would stay and hunt by myself for the next couple of days. It had been a fun start to the hunt; we had gotten close to a few elk and heard a lot of bugles; so although I was sad to see him go, I at least knew he had had fun. He had a trailer, so we stayed in it the last couple of days, we packed up his equipment, and he helped me put up my tent that I would call home for a few days. There was a little town just up the road with a restaurant, so I said I would take him to lunch.

I am not much of a road hunter. I pretty much don't road hunt, but I think you never know when or where you will see an animal. This year, in particular, I had an elk and a deer tag, which doubled my chances of shooting if I did see something. Plus, if I shot something on the way out, my friend could take it into town to the cooler. So I packed up my bow into its case and put it in the back seat of my truck. The road to this location is well maintained. It has a few twists and turns, but it is an easy drive in and out. The first part of the drive from camp goes up a pretty steep incline with a burn scar on the left side of the road.

I am driving up the road at a fair clip and looked to my left, and there, standing less than fifty yards off the road, are two beautiful mule deer bucks. They were both very nice bucks and would have been trophies by anyone's standard. I stopped the truck, figuring they would leave, but they stayed there. So I got out of the truck, opened the back door very quietly, slowly opened my bow case and looked back, and they were still there. At about this time, I realize I might shoot my biggest deer right out of my truck with a bow. I began to get excited. I pulled my bow out, put my release on, and looked again. They were still there. I was shocked.

There was a small berm about six feet high that I would have to climb up to get a shot off, so I climbed up the shelf, fully expecting the bucks to run off the minute they saw me. I peeked over the top of the berm, and they were both still there. I was going to pull this off. I got into a good spot, reached for my arrow. It was at this point that my heart began to sink. You see, I had forgotten my quiver. It was still in the back seat of my truck. Without thinking, I backed away, crawled back down the berm, and grabbed my quiver. To my surprise, the deer were still there. I crawled back up the berm, crested the top. With the flick of an ear and the turn of a head, the bucks shot off up the mountain at full bounds. I was devastated. I could have easily shot one of those two bucks had I just remembered to bring the arrows with me. I had remembered everything that I needed to get the job done, but I forgot, in essence, the most crucial part—the arrow that would do the job.

Quivers come in all shapes and sizes today. You can get a quiver that goes over your back, you can get a quiver that will strap to your leg, and you can get the most common one in hunting, which attaches to your bow. Quivers will hold any number of arrows, I have seen quivers that hold as many as ten arrows, and I have seen quivers that hold as few as two. Of course, there are reasons for any of these various configurations, which are pretty varied. I like a low-profile quiver that will not catch the wind, but I also like the idea of having enough arrows so that if I happen to take a shot and miss, I will have other arrows to use. It doesn't mean I don't find that arrow that I missed with, but I put it back in the quiver so that when I get back to camp, I can look at it and make sure it will still shoot right.

There is a fundamental reason why I share that little tidbit with you. This chapter will deal with what a full quiver looks like, and I don't want someone thinking that a full quiver is some set number of children that we should all have so that we are living biblical principles to the fullest. I also want you to realize that the quiver was—and is—an essential instrument in the field. The quiver does a lot regardless of its stature. It provides a place of readiness. The arrows in the quiver are ready to be shot. It protects the broadhead, so the elements will not dull it. It would protect the archer by covering the broadheads. If the archer were to fall, he would not impale himself. A good quiver will keep the arrow secure so it doesn't fall out and get lost. Finally, the quiver is where the arrow waits until the archer is ready to send it off to a target. These are all critical points because you have to understand the role of the quiver before you can understand this sentence.

I have so many things to say about this sentence "Blessed is the man whose quiver is full of them." Since it is my book, I get to say them. I hope you understand that my goals are not to prove I am right but to point out again that as Christians, we have responsibilities and that we cannot forget our commitments and expect that God will continue to bless us.

The Bible is very clear about the role of children in his kingdom. In Genesis 1:28, God tells us to

> Be fruitful and increase in number, fill the earth and subdue it. Rule over the fish of the sea and the birds in the sky and over every living creature that moves on the ground.

Psalm 128:3 equates children to wealth by calling them olive shoots. Jesus expresses the importance of children in Matthew 18:2–4, which says,

> He called a little child to Him and placed the child among them and said, "Truly I tell you, unless you change and become like little

children, you will never enter the Kingdom of
Heaven. Therefore, whoever takes the lowly position of this child is the greatest in the kingdom of
heaven. And whoever welcomes one such child in
my name welcomes me. If anyone causes one of
these little ones—those who believe in me—to
stumble, it would be better for them to have a
large millstone hung around their neck and be
drowned into the depths of the sea."

The Bible is very clear about children as a blessing. Abraham
receives a blessing in Genesis 22:15. It says,

The angel of the Lord called to Abraham
from heaven a second time and said, "I swear by
myself," declares the Lord, "that because you have
done this and not withheld your son, your only
son, I will surely bless you and make your descendants as numerous as the stars in the sky and as
the sand on the seashore. Your descendants will
take possession of the cities of their enemies, and
through your offspring all nations on earth will
be blessed, because you obeyed me."

Hannah is blessed with more children after she gave Samuel
up, and we know that Mary and Joseph had more children. There is
never a verse that says children are a curse.

So where does that leave this sentence "Blessed is the man
whose quiver is full of them"? Well, I think it means that we are to
have children. I think it means we are to have as many as we can, and
we should be doing that even today.

I know all the reasons not to have many children; I have heard
them all, and I have even discussed them in this book already. But let

me go through some of them for the sake of this chapter and maybe add some more.

1. They are expensive. Amen, I cannot agree with this more. Many sources say it costs $233,000 to raise a child from birth to age 18, and that doesn't include college.
2. The world is so dangerous. I also agree with this statement. It is hard to watch the news and see what is happening and not agree.
3. They take away your freedom. Sure, you lose a lot of liberties when you have children.
4. The world already has too many people in it. Once again, I can't agree more. There are many people in the world, and maybe we don't need to continue to overpopulate it.

The list could keep going. I once read a post called "100 reasons not to have kids," and just so you know, I could come up with many reasons to not have children. They are all, in my opinion, selfish. Let me give simple answers to the statements above. Kids are expensive. This statement, although correct, is misguided because if the Lord builds the house, then he will provide everything we need. So many large families have stories of amazing ways in which God has provided for them. Reason number 2: the world is so dangerous. You are correct. Because of sin, the world is a terrifying and dangerous place, but if the Lord watches over the city, he will watch over us; and even though bad things will still happen, we can be sure that he is protecting us. Objection number 3: you will lose your freedom. Freedom to do what? If the Lord builds the house and the Lord watches over the city, then you will receive the rest you need, take vacations, romantic weekend getaways—whatever you need, God will provide. Last: the world already has too many people in it. The question again comes back to *who* is in charge of the world. You don't think God can do something about resources or overpopulation? Of course, he can. I don't want to be crass here. There are good reasons to be done having children or never have them at all such as health and age, but all of that is put in motion and determined by God, not us. Maybe this idea offends you slightly, and I am not trying to. I want it clear that this particular sentence clearly shows that we are to raise children.

The next part that I want to address in this sentence is to go back to the arrows and their placement in the quiver. In verse 4, the writer clearly shows through the illustration of the arrows that it is the job of the warrior to prep the arrows for use. The warrior nurtures and cares for the arrows from their infant stage (branch) to their adult stage (arrow), it is only when the arrow is ready to be shot that it goes into the quiver. In the quiver, it waits until the warrior has a target for it, and only then is it released.

I fell in love with this analogy when I looked at the idea of what goes in the quiver. The quiver is not full of half-developed arrows that are still being worked on. It is full of arrows that are ready for battle. So, there are a few things that this says to me about raising children:

1. The quiver is full of arrows, ready to go to battle. Whether you have one, two, or twenty children doesn't matter. The goal of everything we do in raising our children is to send them off to battle. The battle that our children fight will be the battle we tell them to fight. Read that again: the battle that our children fight will be the battle we tell them to fight. We have to share with them the conflicts that are worth fighting. I am not here to tell you what action you should prepare your children for, but in my house, the battle is winning souls. We design our children to share the gospel. There is no more important fight in the world, in my opinion. That doesn't have to be your fight, but let me reiterate, you will lead your children to battle, and they will be prepared to fight. Make sure you have taught them which war you want them to fight.

2. The quiver remains with you: This is an important thing that the analogy of the quiver teaches us. When I am hunting, I have my quiver usually. Remember the story at the beginning of the chapter? My quiver is full of fully functional arrows, and if I shoot one and miss the mark, I get it

so that I can put it back in the quiver. Our parenting journey doesn't end when our children are adults or when they have kids of their own or when they are highly successful; it is quite the contrary. Children, like arrows, must always be brought back to the quiver. A good archer doesn't just shoot arrows off and let them land and leave them there. The adult child who gets released into the world and doesn't hit the target doesn't just get left. It is the warrior's job to go and find that arrow (child), brush off the junk, and put it back in the quiver. Children take a lot of work to get in the quiver, and they are vital. It is the job of those raising the children to make sure that if they miss the target, we are there to help them analyze why and make adjustments to hit the target.

3. The quiver is only empty when the final task is complete. If we have done a good job of being involved in our community, our quiver will never be empty. I will focus on the church here. Everyone in the church should be on task with raising children—children that will fight the battle ahead of them. The battle the church has to fight is with the devil, plain and simple. The only way the church wins that battle is to effectively raise a generation of gospel spreaders, broadcasting the seed in every direction possible. The church cannot do that as well as it should if it worries about financial bottom lines and successful retirements. The church must encourage our young couples to have children, and then the church must provide a place for our young parents not to be overwhelmed but instead be lifted up so that they can have a quiver full of battle-ready warriors; then the church will be primed to see revival in the land.

This sentence is clear about three things, and I want to reiterate them before we move on. This sentence makes it very clear that we are supposed to raise children. If you cannot have children biologically, adopt, get involved in your local children's ministry, or help out in community organizations for children. Just realize, you do not get to say, "I am not equipped." One of the jobs God has given us is to raise children. It also makes it clear that having children is not the most critical issue. It is raising the children that holds the most importance. The sentence says, "Blessed is the man whose quiver is full of them." The amount of children does not bless him. He is blessed by the finished arrows, ready to go to battle. Finally, the goal of raising the children is to send them out. A warrior never keeps the arrows in the quiver; the arrows are there for a purpose and must be released to their target, or they are just pretty sticks with sharp points. Ornaments never do anything but hang out. It is the job of the warrior/parent to make sure that the arrows are released.

Chapter 12

The Ethics Matter

They will not be put to shame when they
contend with their opponents in court.
—Psalm 127:5b

A deer hunt is nothing to sneeze at. Although I would rather hunt elk than anything else, I love to hunt deer as well, and drawing a tag in a unit I like and getting to chase them around can be a lot of fun. One year Harmony drew a tag with Jim and me for one of those fun hunts in November. We were all very excited to go and hunt. We used the early fall to get our guns sighted in and make sure we knew where we would be opening morning. Harmony was ready to go out and shoot a deer.

Opening morning came, we had decided to just hunt from home on this trip, which I do a lot on deer hunts because I tend to stay pretty close to home. Jim showed up at the house at about 4:00 a.m., and we started driving out to the spot we were going to hunt. We talked. The whole trip up, Jim and I would share hunting stories, and Harmony would listen and ask questions. Some of the best conversations I have ever had with my children come on trips like this. As we got closer to our spot, I could tell Harmony was getting excited. It wasn't her first hunting trip, but I think we all felt this would be an excellent opportunity to harvest her first animal.

We arrived at our spot a good forty-five minutes before the legal shooting light. We quietly got out of the truck, took the rifles out, loaded them, grabbed all of the gear we would need. This spot wasn't a huge spot, so we didn't grab a ton of equipment. Jim and I had our backpacks, but we told Harmony to leave her stuff at the truck so that she wouldn't be hindered by anything. We still had about thirty minutes before the legal shooting light, so we just stood there, waiting for the light to come up. With about fifteen minutes until legal light, we started to get away from the road a bit in case any deer were moving through the area. We crept, taking our time, making sure the wind was at our face, and being as quiet as we could. We decided to go around some trees to see an opening that we had spotted on our maps. We snuck around those trees and peaked around the corner, and sure enough, two nice mule deer bucks were standing about seventy yards away. Harmony was ready.

Now let me tell you a little bit about New Mexico hunting laws. During this hunt, the law stated that *legal* shooting light was sunrise—not thirty minutes before but sunrise. As we looked at those deer, I told Harmony that it wasn't legal to shoot them. We would have to wait a few minutes, but they hadn't seen us, and I thought it might be okay. It was five minutes before it would be legal to shoot, and when you need deer to stay put for five minutes, likely they won't. They were gone before it was legal to shoot them. We spent the rest of the day hunting that little area and saw nothing but does.

Harmony was pretty upset. She could have easily shot either one of those bucks, and there was enough light to do it. I explained to her that I was upset as well. I always felt that the law was written poorly since I believe the thirty minutes before sunrise to be the best time to hunt, but the law is the law, and we agreed to abide by those laws when we bought our tags.

This situation was difficult for Harmony. She still mentions it today especially since a few short years later, the game and fish changed the shooting time to thirty minutes before sunrise. There are times I do wish that I would have let her shoot that deer. When I tell that story to friends and hunting buddies, they tell me that I was dumb for not letting Harmony shoot that buck. Maybe, but you see,

I don't hunt for the kill. I hunt for the hunt. I think that the lesson I taught Harmony that day was an important one. We need to follow the rules. I passed up a large bull several years ago because it was very close to being too late to shoot, and I didn't want to wound the animal. Ultimately, I would rather have my children enjoy the hunt and make sure that the kill they are making is as ethical as possible. I got to see it in action last year when my son had his cow elk tag. We had several elk on a thick hillside that Nehemiah did not take the shot in because he just couldn't get a good shot. I was frustrated he didn't shoot an elk but proud that he would not take a shot he wasn't 100% sure of.

This story brings us to the last sentence of this passage, and I think it is a tremendous truth that concludes this whole passage so well: "They will not be put to shame when they contend with their opponents in court." This sentence is a statement about the children. The whole passage concludes with the idea that the arrows that have been raised will be pillars in the community and will stand up for their beliefs. They will live lives similar to their families and will be ready to take on the world. This sentence ties up everything quite nicely.

There is a story in the Bible that illustrates this truth very well and is a story many of us have heard. It is the story of Ruth. The story of Ruth goes like this: Elimilek and his wife, Naomi, moved to Moab with their two sons, Mahlon and Kilion. Shortly after they moved to Moab, Elimilek died and left Ruth with her two sons. Her two sons eventually got married to two Moabite women, Ruth and Orpah. After about ten years, Mahlon and Kilion died, leaving Ruth without her husband and two sons. This was not a good situation for Ruth, so she decided to go home.

The Bible says that Naomi prepared to go home and left with her two daughters-in-law. Naomi said to her daughters-in-law in Ruth 1:8,

Go back, each of you, to your mother's home. May the Lord show kindness to you as you have shown kindness to your dead husbands

and to me. May the Lord grant that each of you
will find rest in the home of another husband.

She then kissed them, and they wept aloud. Both daughters told
Naomi that they would go back with her to her land, but Naomi told
them it just didn't make sense. Naomi said to them that she was too
old to have another husband for them to marry, and even if she got
married today and had a son tomorrow, Ruth and Orpah wouldn't
wait for him to grow up, so they needed to go home and find a husband. Orpah decided to go home, but Ruth did not. She says in Ruth
1:16–17,

> Don't urge me to leave you or turn back
> from you. Where you go I will go, and where you
> stay I will stay. Your people will be my people and
> your God, my God. Where you die I will die, and
> there I will be buried.

Naomi realizes that Ruth is coming with her, and they both go
to Bethlehem.

The rest of the story is one of the most amazing stories in the
Bible. Naomi and Ruth were single women who had no family to
take care of them, so it says Ruth would go out and gather the left-
over grain after the harvesters went through. The field that she would
do this in was Boaz's, who was a relative of Naomi. The way it is
written, it doesn't sound like Boaz's field was picked by Ruth on purpose, but Boaz was impressed. He told Ruth not to go into any other
field, that Ruth should only glean from his field. When Ruth asked
why she had found favor with him, Boaz told her how he had heard
about all Ruth had done for Naomi, leaving her own family to care
for her mother-in-law. She was allowed to eat dinner there, take leftovers with her, and gather more grain. By the time she went home, it
says she had an Ephah, which is probably about thirty pounds. She
gave the grain to Naomi and the leftovers. Naomi was moved by the
amount she had brought. She asked Ruth, "Where did you glean
today? Blessed be the man who took notice of you!" When Ruth told

her whose field she had been working, Naomi explained to Ruth who Boaz was and told Ruth to stay close to Boaz's field and that she would be safe there because he was such a close relative. Ruth did precisely that.

Naomi was determined to take care of her daughter-in-law. The plan was that Ruth would gain favor with Boaz and that he would marry Ruth. This plan was a pretty long one. I won't go into details, but it involved perfume, nice clothes, and bare feet. If you want to read it, it can be found in the book of Ruth, a good read. The plan worked, and Ruth and Boaz were married. Soon after they were married, Ruth had a son. His name was Obed, who was the father of Jesse, who was the father of David. Because of her faithfulness to Naomi, Ruth ends up being the great-grandmother to the king of Israel, which is also the family tree of Jesus. What a tremendous blessing.

In most cases, people give all the credit to Ruth in this story, and rightly so, she acted in a very sacrificial way. She could have gone home. I think that Naomi doesn't get enough credit here. Naomi must have been an amazing mother-in-law for both her daughters-in-law not to want to leave her. There is a lesson here that fits with the last sentence of our passage: "They will not be put to shame when they contend with their opponents in court." This story shares some excellent insight into this. First of all, Naomi had earned Ruth's loyalty. Even though they were not blood relatives, Ruth was determined to care for her mother-in-law. Ruth chose Naomi over her own home. I think this says a lot about Naomi's ability to raise arrows. She had spent about ten years with Ruth. Naomi had a significant impact on Ruth. Second, Naomi had respect in her hometown. When she returned home, people did not shun her, and Ruth must have seen how people treated her when they went back to Jerusalem. The last thing is that Ruth obeyed Naomi. Naomi had lived a life and showed through example that she knew what was best for Ruth.

I use the story of Ruth for several reasons. Ruth shows that just because a child is not yours doesn't mean you cannot significantly affect their lives. Maybe you are a stepparent, a foster parent, a family friend, a teacher, a pastor, a volunteer, or even an in-law. You can be a warrior that raises children to contend at the courts. This story also shows that the raising doesn't quit when the child becomes an adult. This story shows me that it wasn't just Ruth who sacrificed. Naomi also sacrificed. Naomi probably wanted to go back to her home, live a simple life, and die a widow. When she decided to take Ruth along, she didn't get to Bethlehem and leave Ruth to fend for herself. She taught Ruth what to do to succeed, and Naomi's plan was indeed successful.

With this sentence, we must realize how critical raising children is. How we raise our children, even into adulthood, will be reflected in how our children act in the community. The lessons we teach them, the actions we show them, and the people we allow into their lives will profoundly affect who they become. Here are a few things I think we should take from this verse:

1. We are never done raising children. No matter how old or successful our children become, they still need us. Whether we are their parents, their mentors, or even their teachers, they need us. They need us always to be good examples. They will do whatever they see us do. One of my biggest pet peeves is when you have marriages that dissolve when the children are out of the house. This idea that says, "Well, we did our job. Now let's be free," is something that bothers me. I have seen many people decide that since their children are adults, they can slack off their disciplines. That is so far from the truth. Our children pay close attention to how we act until we die. We are always raising our children.

2. Raising children is about raising adults. The goal of raising children has to be that we not just get to adulthood but through adulthood. I know this is similar to the first point, but I want you to realize that little eyes decide what specific behaviors they repeat as adults at an early age. If we are angry at our children, they will understand that to be a valid adult behavior. If we spend our time on foolish behaviors, our children will see those behaviors as normal. Understand that as adults, we are shapers and developers

of the children. They are watching, and they will do what they see us do.

3. Unless the Lord. If we are raising our children with the solid foundation of the Lord, our children will likely have that foundation when they are older. The children we raise are a reflection of us. If we are not a reflection of the Lord, we cannot expect our children to be.

The children we raise will be a part of the community, have jobs, have their own children, and talk about us. They will reflect everything we have taught them, good and bad. When they are adults, and they are doing their various life activities, they will let others know about the things we taught them. How do you want them to talk? I think that this last sentence gives us a worthy goal. I will take it one step further—how will they talk about God? I hope that the children I have raised will always speak highly of the Lord and, in turn, will speak highly of me because "unless the Lord."

Chapter 13

A Legacy

As soon as I saw Ron, I knew I was home. Ron is a dear friend of my dad's. They have known each other since before I was born. Ron is friendly, he is a good friend, and I have always enjoyed our conversations. So I was excited to spend the next few hours with him as we drove to elk camp. The drive to camp would take us about four or five hours, so the conversation should be rich. It was a nice drive, and I was excited when we finally got to camp. Opening day was the next day, and I was there, hunting with my dad and brother. It had been a long time since I had been able to do that, so I was excited even though I didn't have a tag. The minute we got there, everyone came out to greet us and help us get our stuff into the tent. When I walked into the tent, I was immediately swept back in time. The canvas smell, the beds—everything about it caused me to feel very comfortable and very much at home. We sat and talked for a while as the fire roared in the woodstove and the radio played music. Stories were shared, and moments were remembered. Soon it was time for us to sleep to be ready to hunt in the morning. I would go with my dad to his stand while everyone else went to theirs.

The morning came pretty fast, the fire stoked, and breakfast cooked. We all ate our breakfast, got dressed for the hunt, and were out the door pretty quick. I felt like a little kid walking behind my dad to his stand. My dad—one of the greatest men I have ever known. He isn't perfect, no one is, but he is a good man. As a child, I don't remember when I needed him that he wasn't there. Even as an adult, he is always available. He coached my baseball teams for my entire childhood, which means he was instrumental in the lives of multiple young men. In my opinion, he can do anything. He could build things, fix things, hunt anything, and make ends meet when you thought it couldn't be done. He taught me how to hunt because he is the best hunter I know. He taught me how to fish because he is the best fisherman I know. He showed me how to be a good friend, not just a friend but also a good friend. He would do anything for anyone. He showed me how to care for people that weren't like me. He was and is an amazing dad. I have tried to emulate him, but I can't; he set the bar too high, and here I was, following in his footsteps yet again, feeling like that little kid trying to step in the footsteps he left. My dad took more time than when I was younger; he moved a little slower, but I was just as excited to get to follow him.

We got to the stand early enough, dad kicked the heater on, and we both settled in for a while to see if any elk would come. We whispered while we watched for elk. I took out my calls and did some calling even though the rut had been over for some time. No elk came by, and it was still fun.

We had been sitting there a while when we began to hear shots fairly close by. There were quite a few shots, and we felt pretty confident that it was one of our guys. Dad said I should head back to camp just in case anyone needed help packing out an elk; Ron stayed in camp with the radio, and if anyone had shot something, he would be able to tell me. I walked back to camp, hoping that someone had had some success. When I got back to camp, Ron said to me that my brother, Mel, had shot a bull and that I could take the radio and help him. I grabbed a couple of game packs, some water, and the radio and headed where Ron told me to go. My family has radios with GPS in them, so as soon as I could talk to Mel, his position showed up, making it easy to find him. I remember being very excited. My brother Mel and me were never really close as kids. He is seven years older than me, so I was more of a pain than a companion. There were many times that Mel had to take me along as he did things a sixteen or seventeen-year-old would do. As we got older, we became closer, we hunted and fished a lot together, and we enjoy each other's company. He is still my older brother, and even though he can be a typical older brother, he is a lot of fun, and he is a great brother. I found Mel about halfway down a very steep canyon, standing over a beautiful five-point bull. He was grinning from ear to ear. I immediately felt joy in getting to be here for this moment with him.

We took a few pictures. I listened to the story of my brother's biggest bull, and we started the work of getting his animal out of the canyon. We were only three hundred yards from camp as the crow flies, but two hundred of those yards were pretty straight up, so this was not going to be easy. It took about one hour to get the first load up, and Dad was there at camp, waiting. Here were two of his sons, packs full of meat, laughing, talking, and just enjoying the moment. At the time, I didn't think about what that might mean to him, but as I write this today, I am sure it is a moment. Indeed, the whole day was one of those days—a day that you will never get to repeat, one of those special days. By the end of the day, I was tired, I was in pain, and I was overjoyed. I could only imagine how my dad felt as everyone celebrated the occasion. He witnessed the legacy left by him, the life of a dedicated man to his children. He was teaching them how to hunt together.

When God moved my family and me away from Oregon, it was not easy. You have seen in this book—at least I hope you have—that my family is an integral part of who I am, and I love them. Moving away didn't seem hard at the time, but I realized just how much I miss them as I have gotten older. Because of that, I try and get back to Oregon more now. This trip was memorable for a lot of reasons, but it also made me realize something about the passage today, and that is this: "What legacy do I want to leave my children?" My dad has left a very definite legacy, and I get to understand that legacy every fall when I go out into the field and chase animals. But I then have to ask what legacy I want to leave for my children?

What about you? I want you to think long and hard about that. Because "unless the Lord" is a great legacy to leave behind.

Unless the Lord builds the house, the builders labor in vain. Are you willing to allow God to do the building? Are you ready to see

God's provision and accept it as a gift? The world says to make more than you need so you can have all that you want. If you go into debt for it, that is fine. Suppose you sacrifice relationships for it, okay. But this passage and many others say it very differently—unless the Lord. The Lord will provide all that you need and more, but you must be willing to let him build the house and provide for you and your family.

Unless the Lord watches over the city, the guards stand watch in vain. Are you worried about your safety? Your family's safety? Are you concerned about your retirement? The world says that we make sure we are watching over all that we have and plan well to not depend on others, insure our investments, and make sure we have enough in case of a disaster. This passage and others like it share the exact opposite. It is not our job to protect our stuff, our children, or even our home, God built it, and he will protect it.

In vain, you rise up early and stay up late, toiling for food to eat? How hard do you work? How much time do you spend worrying about your future, your things, your investments, and your self-worth? The world says sacrifice everything to get ahead so that you can have more, but this passage says it is all in vain. The Lord says that he takes care of the birds and the flowers, and we are more important than them. Why do we toil when God provides the food?

He grants sleep to those he loves. Do you stay up at night worried about what will happen if? If you lose everything? If your child dies? If your marriage ends? The world says that we must do everything in our power to achieve success, and sleep is not essential as long as you are building your self-worth. This passage is clear that rest is given to those he loves, and the Bible says he loves everyone and sent his son down so that all who believe in him would not perish but have everlasting life.

If you are willing to let God provide and let God protect you, you will have all you need and be provided for even in your sleep.

Children are a heritage from the Lord, offspring a reward from him. The world says children are a burden, a hassle, and we should avoid having them as long as possible if we have them at all. This passage tells us that children are his heritage and reward, and we should want a reward. We shouldn't see them as anything but that.

Like arrows in the hands of a warrior are the children of one's youth. The world says wait to have children so that you have the means to get them everything they could ever want. This passage says having children is only the start. The goal is to raise arrows, ready to go to battle. The younger we have them, the more time we get to mold them.

Blessed is the man whose quiver is full of them. The world says to keep your family small so that you can continue to live your life to the fullest. Don't have too many children, and don't spend too much time on them. This passage says raise your children so that they can continue the good fights and that they are meant to be released into the world.

They will not be put to shame when they contend with their opponents in court. The world says get your children to adulthood and stop raising them. This passage says to be involved in raising your children for as long as you can. Make your children proud so that they will be your defenders.

Conclusion

As I look outside my window today, I am looking at a green desert; it gets me excited for my deer hunt this fall. I know that the deer will have had plenty of nutrients to grow big antlers, and they will be fat and lots of meat. I know that there will be enough water that will keep them moving, but more than all of it, I will enjoy walking through the long grass that doesn't always greet us here in New Mexico. When I think about hunting, I think about family, and I think about the Lord. I know that successful hunting requires many factors, but the most essential factor is the Lord. My dad always says hunting is 90 percent "right place right time." If the Lord decides I will be successful, I will. The same is true of life.

There are many factors in life. When it comes to family, those factors multiply. However you grew up, and however you have decided to live your life, do it to the fullest. I make some pretty clear thoughts about what I think about marriage and parenting in this book. I hope you don't come to the end of this book and decide, "I am selling everything, having as many kids as I can, and living in a shack." I wouldn't want anyone to do that. Instead, I want you to start evaluating everything you do with one thought in mind—"unless the Lord":

> Unless the Lord builds the house,
> the builders labor in vain.
> Unless the Lord watches over the city,
> the guards stand watch in vain.
> In vain you rise early

131

and stay up late,
toiling for food to eat—
for He grants sleep to those He loves.
Children are a heritage from the Lord,
offspring a reward from him.
Like arrows in the hands of a warrior
are children born in one's youth.
Blessed is the man
whose quiver is full of them.
They will not be put to shame
when they contend with their opponents in court.

The concept of this passage is not to narrow you into one way of life but instead broaden it, to ask questions and adjust your way of thinking. Know this. I don't want you to believe that the only way to follow the Lord is by doing everything I have done. Please don't think that; I have made and still make many mistakes. I just want you to constantly be asking the question, "Why do I do what I do?" Because unless the Lord is the driving force behind your decisions, you will not find the joy you are looking for. Allow the Lord to be your sole provider and your sole protector. Allow him to help you decide your family size and structure, and remember that he loves you and that he wants more for you than you could ever imagine.

Unless the Lord.

About the Author

Alan Gedde grew up in the Pacific Northwest and now lives in the dry Southwest. He has been married for twenty-nine years to the love of his life, and they have six children together. He went to Southwestern Baptist College, now Arizona Christian University, for his undergrad and received his master's degree at Wayland Baptist University. He has served as a youth pastor, music pastor, and interim senior pastor. Currently, he is the children's pastor at Grace Community Church in Roswell, New Mexico, where he ministers to the children in the community.

All of these different roles have allowed Alan to develop a love for the families he sees. Because of this love, Alan has a desire to see families become stronger and happier. He wants to see children grow up in homes where God is the foundation and becomes the foundation of their lives.

Alan is an avid hunter. Whenever hunting season comes around, you will find Alan in the woods or on the plains chasing his quarry.